DINING IN
FRANCE

by Christian Millau

photographs by Philippe-Louis Houzé

SIDGWICK & JACKSON
LONDON

Photographs preceding frontispiece:
Geese, raised for their livers, in Périgord.
Joigny, on the Loire.
Fresh strawberries at a Joigny market.
Red velvet banquette at Le Grand Véfour.
Frontispiece: Some ingredients of
Andre Daguin's foie gras dishes.

Design by J.C. Suarès
Text translated by Sheila Mooney Mall.
Directed by André Gayot.
Recipes translated, tested, and adapted by
Harriet Reilly and Tina Ujlaki.
Captions by Elizabeth Powers.

First published in Great Britain in 1986
by Sidgwick & Jackson Ltd.

First Published in the United States in 1986
by Stewart, Tabori & Chang, Inc., New York

ISBN 0 283 99395 2

Printed and bound in Italy
by Arnoldo Mondadori Editore, Verona
for Sidgwick & Jackson Ltd.
1 Tavistock Chambers, Bloomsbury Way
London WC1A 2SG

When using the recipes in this book it is important
to note that the metric and imperial measurements
given are not interchangeable.

Jacques Maximin
Chantecler (Hôtel Negresco)

Georges Blanc

Jacques Chibois
Le Royal-Gray

CONTENTS

Alain Chapel

Michel Trama
L'Aubergade

Pierre Gagnaire
Saint-Etienne

INTRODUCTION by PIERRE SALINGER

GREAT CHEFS. FINE FOOD. Superb wines. Three hundred and sixty-five different cheeses. Champagne, a bubbly wine that has become the symbol of celebration. Scores of regions, attached to their past and their differences from the rest of France. All these are elements that make up the extraordinary diversity and quality of dining in France.

When the idea was first proposed to me of doing a television series on the subject, I wanted to go further than just making a tour of the greatest restaurants in France. They are, of course, part of the story. But in order to understand dining in France, you also have to know something about its past, its present, and its future.

France is the birthplace and kingdom of gastronomy. From the days of the Greco-Roman empire, through the Middle Ages, the era of Kings, the French Revolution, the Empire, through until today, the evolution of French food and the manner in which it is presented has been striking. That evolution is linked to history and to families who have passed down special talents from generation to generation. We set out to do the series and this book at the same time and spent almost a year travelling around

Michel Rostang

Bernard Loiseau
Hôtel de la Côte d'Or

Louis Outhier
L'Oasis

France. We met the great chefs such as Pierre Troisgros, Paul Bocuse, Jacques Maximin, Georges Blanc, Roger Vergé, and Alain Senderens. And through them we learned about their styles, about the way they choose their foods and wines, about their conceptions of cooking.

A real chef is a whole organization. Take Pierre Troisgros, who with his now deceased brother, Jean, founded a restaurant in the central French town of Roanne, just across the street from the railroad station. (The station is specially painted in pink and green to match one of the Troisgros specialties—Le Saumon à l'Oseille—salmon with sorell). Troisgros has a special producer for his cheeses, for his wines, for his special French Charolais beef. I was able to visit the Troisgros restaurant and hotel, and watch the smooth workings of a not-so-simple operation.

In Vonnas, the young Georges Blanc, who took over the restaurant La Mère Blanc from his mother when he was still in his twenties, took me to see how they raise the very special Bresse chicken; the raising of *poulet de bresse* is carefully controlled to produce high quality. In Nice, at the Hôtel Negresco, Jacques Maximin, an artist of desserts, taught me how chocolate can play a key role in a superb French meal. In Reims, Gerard Boyer, now installed in the historic Château des Crayères, told me the history of Champagne, and how each brand is a blend of wines mixed to a certain taste. In Paris I visited Androuet, the most famous cheese dealer in France, and went through his incredible caves where almost all of France's three hundred and sixty-five cheeses are prepared for sale or delivery to top restaurants. And to conclude the show I went to the second floor of the Eiffel Tower in Paris to the new haute cuisine restaurant, the Jules Verne—a combination of great food and an exceptional view of the city.

Our year of dining in France was a very special adventure that we attempt to communicate through television and in book form. This volume will be a valuable asset if you really want to know about dining in France.

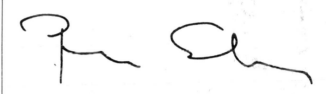

Pierre Salinger
Paris
February 1986

Gérard Boyer
Château des Crayères

Claude Deligne with
Jean-Claude Vrinat
Taillevent

Paul and Marc Haeberlin
Auberge de l'Ill

their colourful plumage, fire spurting from their beaks. In medieval times, the royal kitchens employed hundreds of people to prepare an extremely elaborate cuisine rivalled only by the ornate dishes served in the halls of the greatest lords. The common folk generally ate simple and rather crude fare: soups, roasts, and the like.

The Renaissance marked the dawn of a new gastronomic era in France. When Catherine de Medici wed the Duke of Orleans (who later became Henry II of France) in 1533, she brought with her to the Louvre (then the royal residence) her own chefs, recipes, even ingredients and spices. The court's heavy and complicated cuisine gave way to simpler, more refined dishes; it was at this time that fish was first prepared in sauce.

French cuisine evolved over time, influenced by fashion and by the personal styles of succeeding sovereigns: Louis XIV (1638–1715), the Sun King, was a glutton; Louis XV (1710–1774) was a refined gourmet. Invariably, however, it was rich food expensively prepared and remained exclusively available to the privileged classes.

At the time of the French Revolution, restaurants began to emerge and French cuisine became available to the public. In the nineteenth century it entered the homes of aristocrats and wealthy bourgeois, all of whom had chefs or at least a cook and a kitchen staff. The most famous chefs cooked in private houses, like Carême, who is known as the Cook of kings and the King of cooks. He worked for Talleyrand, Napoleon's foreign minister, and for the Prince Regent in England. Today, although few French families employ kitchen staffs, grande cuisine is available to anyone in restaurants, with only the prices protecting its exclusive status.

The grande cuisine of the nineteenth and first half of the twentieth century is known as *classic cuisine*. A cookbook by the famed chef Auguste Escoffier, which was published early in this century, defined the classic method in detail and remained a bible for chefs for decades. But by the 1960s, classic cuisine had entered a period of decline. Taste was sacrificed to appearance. Rich and costly ingredients, such as foie gras, caviar, and truffles, were ubiquitous. Bad habits—leaving stockpots long on the back burner, preparing dishes in advance and reheating them—were common, and France's gastronomic reputation became sadly tarnished. Some restaurants survived solely on past glories and prepared food the way they did fifty years ago, such as Point in Vienne, not far from Lyons, or Le Père Bise in Talloires on the Lac d'Annecy, to mention only the most famous.

Most classic grande cuisine preparations have by now vanished from the menus of renowned restaurants: in truth, the dogmatic classic cuisine was generally better to look at than to eat. *Nouvelle cuisine* is an approach to cooking that emerged at the beginning of the 1970s in reaction to classic cuisine. It freed the creative inspiration of young chefs who had felt bound by Escoffier's rules. Within fifteen years, its guiding principles became part of the French culinary heritage, and they continue to inspire the best dishes in the best restaurants.

Nouvelle cuisine advocated a few simple practices that seemed to correspond to changing tastes. People began to demand lighter food in keeping with their concern for health and fitness. There was a trend towards simplicity and the use of fresh products and seasonal ingredients; shortened cooking times allowed vegetables and fish to retain their natural flavours and nutrients. Lightness became the new watchword, with alcohol, flour, butter, cream, and fat avoided entirely or kept at a minimum.

Menus grew smaller, which meant restaurants no longer had to keep stocks of unused food in the refrigerator. The menus also changed often, to make use of seasonal products and reflect the chef's latest inspiration. This new emphasis on personal artistry encouraged experiments and welcomed influences from regional cooking and from abroad—particularly from Asian cuisine. New kitchen technologies, such as food processors and microwave ovens, were adopted as well.

The look of dining itself changed. Large plates, called "American plates" in France, allowed chefs to arrange food in an appetizing way and avoid unintentional mixtures. The philosophy of nouvelle cuisine is that the experience of dining should be totally pleasurable, with the presentation of the food and refinement of the table setting complementing the quality and sophistication of the cuisine.

Regional, or *rustic, cooking* includes many centuries-old traditions. In France, every sixty miles produces a new region with not only its own architecture and landscape but also its own cooking. The richness and diversity of regional cooking give the French a fantastically complex culinary heritage. Yet because the modern world tends to reduce this diversity, most people today eat the same kind of food whether they live in Provence or Brittany. Restaurants have become the preservers of culinary traditions and nowadays there is a significant trend towards a return to regional roots. Although some restaurateurs on the Riviera, for instance, serve canned fish soup, and some in Alsace serve little but sauerkraut, more and more restaurants are searching out forgotten local recipes and offering a gastronomic panorama of their region. Nearly all French regional specialties can be had in Paris, but the best place to sample them is on their home turf where the finest products are grown and local cooks prepare them.

In Paris, *bistro cuisine* is also called *cuisine bourgeoise* because it is the kind of cooking people would traditionally eat every day. Because it consists chiefly of long-simmered dishes requiring a good deal of time to prepare, bourgeois cooking these days is less often to be found in the home than in little restaurants. It is generous fare, sometimes a bit heavy, but perfectly delicious when made well. The most well known bourgeois specialties are dishes like pot-au-feu (boiled beef), navarin d'agneau (lamb stew), daube de boeuf (beef stew), hachis Parmentier (meat and potato hash), tête de veau sauce gribiche (calf's head with a mayonnaise sauce), boeuf mode (beef stew), stuffed cabbage, leg of lamb with garlic, grilled pig's trotters, lapin chasseur (rabbit with tomato and mushroom sauce), mouton aux haricots blancs (mutton stew with white beans), raie au beurre noir or noisette (skate with browned butter), and grilled sole. An excellent lamb stew is in fact served to the staff at Lasserre, although it is not considered elegant enough to be listed on the menu!

19

The famous, rich ingredients of French grande cuisine were all once produced in France, but the industrialization of the countryside has meant that many types of produce have died out or become scarce. Once exclusively French products now come from all over the world.

The famed "Périgord truffles" have almost totally vanished from Périgord, in the department of Dordogne, although they are unearthed in the neighbouring Lot region and more often still in the department of Vaucluse, in the Rhône Valley. Today's truffle crop is four times smaller than at the turn of the century, while demand keeps growing. Nearly fifty percent of the French truffle production is in fact Spanish. And since they are absolutely indistinguishable, truffles from across the border are quite legally labelled Périgord truffles.

Frogs have become so rare that most served in restaurants are imports from Poland, Turkey, Yugoslavia, or Bangladesh. Most of the famed "Burgundy snails" come from Eastern Europe. Foie gras is so much in demand that small French farms cannot raise fatted geese fast enough; almost half of the foie gras canned in France originates in Bulgaria, Israel, or Hungary. Crayfish are imported from Poland and Yugoslavia, pigs from East Germany and China, tomatoes from the Netherlands, green beans from Senegal, lobsters from South Africa. But if people are ready to pay the price and to go to a bit of trouble, it is still possible to find ingredients of French origin. In fact, the level of quality has risen in a pretty spectacular way.

Manners and customs in France are not so different from those in English-speaking countries, but subtle differences do exist. Dinner is later and more leisurely, for example, and dress is generally more formal. Restaurant personnel—especially the head waiter and sommelier—are members of a professional elite, and their advice should be respected, though it need not be followed. Familiarity with a few French traditions will ensure a memorable dining experience.

Reservations. One must make dinner reservations far in advance at the more celebrated restaurants in Paris and from May to December in the top provincial establishments. Many restaurants have grown wary of reservations from abroad; too many customers have forgotten to cancel their reservations and simply not shown up, leaving the restaurants with an empty table for the evening. Sending a check for about twenty pounds with a letter or making a credit card deposit through a travel agent, however, will

woman carried to his table on a silver platter; another eccentric made his entrance on a horse; and Ivan, the Grand Duke of Russia, finished eight bottles of Mumm Champagne, then sank to the floor in a stupor. World War I put an end to such follies; during the 1930s, Maxim's was simply the most elegant restaurant in Paris, perhaps in the world. During the Occupation, German officers merrily quaffed Maxim's Champagne. In the 1960s and 70s, after an eclipse, Maxim's recovered its prestige. On a given evening, seated side by side on what was dubbed the "Royal Banquette" (five tables numbered 16 to 20), current royalty could be seen: Jackie Onassis and Maria Callas, the Duke and Duchess of Windsor, the Maharani of Baroda dripping with diamonds, and Grace and Rainier of Monaco. Albert, the portly director, seated his guests according to their wealth or celebrity; newcomers were greeted with an icy glance that could cow the stoutest heart. But gradually, the movers and shakers dropped in less frequently or else vanished altogether and the customary Friday black-tie dinners fell into disuse.

In the early 1980s, Louis Vaudable, who had owned Maxim's for almost half a century, decided to retire. Who would take on this endangered monument, with its staff of 110 employees, its 200,000-bottle wine cellar, its huge operating expenses, and its outdated kitchens? Pierre Cardin, already a stockholder in the restaurant, was an unlikely saviour. The famous couturier took over Maxim's partly for the fun of it, and partly to give Paris a new sense of festivity. The first thing he did was to have it cleaned. (Paul Bocuse, who once worked in Maxim's kitchens, swears that he used to chase rats there!) At the sumptuous re-opening gala in 1982, Cardin's guests discovered a newly resplendent Maxim's. In the large ground-floor dining room, which featured an orchestra and the famous Royal Banquette, the glass roof and famous murals had recovered their former colour and luminosity. The first-floor dining room and bar, "L'Impériale," had been entirely re-done with Art Nouveau period furniture. The second-floor salons, used for receptions, cocktail parties, and private dinners, were redecorated with

extraordinary attention to detail: a mahogany bar, stained glass windows with wisteria motifs, polychromed cornices, bevelled mirrors, pink lamps, and wall murals.

Overnight, Maxim's once again became a beacon in the nightlife of Paris. Evening dress is now de rigueur on Fridays, and Pierre Cardin often throws elaborate parties to honour his friends from the worlds of opera, dance, film, or art. Lunch hour at Maxim's is no longer deserted; midday meals in the Garden Room—a kind of conservatory, with a glass wall that affords a view of the Rue Royale—are among the liveliest in Paris. A dinner table in the Grande Salle, beneath the glass roof, must be reserved at least a week in advance. Celebrities are seated, naturally, on the Royal Banquette; the less-well-known are directed to the left side; the rest to the right and the middle of the room in front of the orchestra. A six-piece band plays current hits in a style that makes rock and roll sound like Viennese waltzes.

Probably no other restaurant in France serves more Champagne than Maxim's. An ice bucket with a bottle of bubbly is automatically placed on every table, though should diners prefer another type of wine, the cellar holds all the best growths (some at staggering prices) as well as modest wines at fairly reasonable prices. Maxim's food has never been its drawing card. Although chef Michel Menant has lots of talent (on advance order, he can prepare exquisite meals), the eclectic menu jumbles together elaborate, outmoded "haute cuisine" (saddle of veal Orloff, pheasant Souvaroff), bourgeois-style cooking (beef in aspic), and other dishes of more modern inspiration (not always the most successful), which gives the cuisine here a somewhat heterogeneous air. It is wise to choose the simplest offerings, like the marvellous warm lobster à la nage, in aromatic broth. Maxim's frequently serves almost five hundred meals a day, but with a staff that includes ten head waiters, fourteen waiters, seventeen busboys, and six wine stewards, service is swift and precise. The new young director, Jean-Pierre Guevel, unlike the notorious Albert, greets every guest with the same warm smile.

La Tour d'Argent is definitely the oldest restaurant in Paris. Founded in 1582, it is said that forks first appeared at table here. For years, owner Claude Terrail, who with his boutonniere and London-tailored suits cuts a dashing figure, steadfastly refused to consider any changes in the food served at La Tour d'Argent. Apparently persuaded that his cuisine was the best in the world, he did not see the need to renew his menu (a handsome piece of work, by the way, with a sumptuous silver cover), which offered dishes that were so rich and so complicated that one sometimes wondered exactly what was on the plate. But when he finally realized that his restaurant was in peril of being permanently out-

Although Dominique Bouchet has presided over a culinary revolution at La Tour d'Argent, he has not removed the restaurant's famous numbered duck from the menu.

stripped by its competitors, he gave carte blanche to his young chef, Dominique Bouchet. Bouchet has accomplished a veritable revolution at La Tour d'Argent.

Most of the pompous preparations wallowing in rich sauces have been replaced by a delicate, refined cuisine that produces marvels like the pâté of lobster in truffle aspic, sautéed langoustines and artichokes seasoned with hazelnut oil, roast salmon with beef marrow, a remarkable leg of lamb braised for several hours with vegetables and then served with a spoon. Bouchet's masterpiece is an old recipe he unearthed: very rare duck breast plunged into boiling, highly spiced broth accompanied by souffléed potatoes.

The tidal wave that swept the menu did spare the famous "duck Tour d'Argent," known throughout the world for almost a century. It was around 1890 that Frédéric, former head waiter and later owner of the restaurant, was inspired to serve a duck in two separate courses: first the breast, covered with a sauce thickened with the animal's blood; afterwards the grilled duck's legs. The true stroke of genius was numbering the ducks and giving each client a card bearing the bird's number. In 1900, Grand Duke Vladimir of Russia consumed duck number 6,043 and on May 16, 1948 the then Princess Elizabeth dined on number 185,387. In 1986, the total approaches 700,000!

In the 1930s, André Terrail, Claude's father, moved the restaurant from the ground floor to the building's top floor, where it is today. The view that the restaurant affords of the Seine and, at night, of Notre Dame bathed in light, draws cries of delight and admiration from first-time patrons; one must reserve fairly far in advance to obtain a table near the picture window. On the ground floor, in the restaurant's former precincts, where the superb original wood panels remain, Claude Terrail exhibits historical memorabilia relating to the restaurant. Diners can inspect this interesting collection and sip an aperitif before entering the elevator that will take them to the top of La Tour. In the display cases are table and kitchen utensils (a sixteenth-century fork, a seventeenth-century coffee mill, a drinking glass that belonged to Empress Elizabeth I of Russia), a superb collection of antique menus, and autographs of famous patrons from President Eisenhower to the present Emperor of Japan. Most impressive is the table at which the "Three Emperors' Dinner" took place on June 7, 1867; it is laid with the same cloth and dishes today. The three were Alexander II, the czar of Russia; the czarevitch Alexander; and William II of Prussia.

To finish the evening, tradition dictates that patrons of La Tour d'Argent descend to the wine cellar for a glass of old Cognac or Armagnac. Nearly 200,000 bottles sleep in the cellar just a few yards from the Seine river bed. These imposing surroundings are the setting for a "sound and light show," narrated by Claude Terrail. A spotlight illuminates in turn each of the most precious bottles in the collection: a Château Citran 1855, a Château d'Yquem 1871, a Chambertin 1865, a Cognac Fine Champagne 1797. Just before World War II, the millionaire Pierpont Morgan had a couple of James Bond types spirit away two bottles of Napoleon Cognac from La Tour d'Argent wine cellar. Although he had offered Terrail a small fortune, the American had not succeeded in persuading him to part with the brandy. In their place, Terrail found a letter of apology and a blank cheque. A good sport, he returned the cheque to Pierpont Morgan, who kept the bottles.

Of all the restaurants that flourished around

the gardens of the Palais-Royal during the Revolution and under Napoleon, only one still stands today, but it is unquestionably one of the loveliest in the world: Le Grand Véfour. In the darkest days of the Terror, Le Grand Véfour was a favourite meeting place for counter-revolutionaries. Later, young General Bonaparte was a regular customer, and until the end of the nineteenth century all the celebrities of the day dined there, from the great gastronome Brillat-Savarin to Victor Hugo. Then decline set in, and the place became just another dingy neighbourhood café. But in the 1950s, a chef from Bordeaux named Raymond Oliver restored some of its former splendor to Le Grand Véfour. Jean Cocteau and Colette, who lived a few steps away, ate there frequently; soon Le Grand Véfour was again a fashionable spot. Thanks to a weekly television cooking show, Raymond Oliver found himself the most famous chef in France, beating even Paul Bocuse in the polls. Like the latter, Oliver took to spending less and less time in his kitchen, cooking virtually only for the camera. By the 1960s the gastronomic reputation of Le Grand Véfour declined, and the restaurant's decor deteriorated at a truly alarming rate. Struck down by illness, Raymond Oliver decided to sell Le Grand Véfour. He had the good fortune to meet up with Jean Taittinger (of the Champagne and the Concorde hotel chain group), who already owned the Hôtel de Crillon and had a great interest in historical sites. Taittinger completely restored the restaurant's glorious original decor, including its painted ceiling and the allegorical murals under glass that date from the reign of Napoleon III.

The atmosphere, at once lively and refined, makes for enchanting luncheons and dinners. A new chef has injected fresh vigour into the cooking as well. André Signoret overhauled and renewed Le Grand Véfour's repertory. Although not an out-and-out modernist, he serves a light cuisine that immediately lured back the chic Parisian clientele. The food is very good (salt cod with celery and bay, bass with mustard garnished with deep-fried fennel, fillet of lamb in a potato cake, veal kidney and sweetbreads with lemon) and served in so exceptional a setting that one easily sees why Le Grand Véfour has had such rousing success.

Before we leave the Taittinger family, we should say a few words about the Crillon. The hotel's restaurant is also, in its way, a historical monument. Its reputation is fairly recent, for a few years ago the hotel had only a grill room. It was decided to convert one of the large salons into a dining room called Les Ambassadeurs. With its marble and trompe l'oeil decorations, the room is a masterpiece, the work of the architect Jacques Gabriel who, under Louis XV, designed and built the Place de la Concorde and the palaces that surround it. The excellent chef, Jean-Paul Bonin, is an advocate of light, modern, inventive cuisine (tomato-stuffed red mullet steamed with basil, prawns in aspic with cabbage, truffled lobster, honeyed lamb with courgette au gratin, numerous and particularly luscious desserts).

The Hôtel Ritz, another historic survivor, enjoyed a world-wide gastronomic reputation early in the century thanks to the celebrated chef, Auguste Escoffier. That reputation is now extinct, however, for the Ritz clings resolutely to its old-fashioned luxury hotel cuisine, which bears no comparison with the food served at the Crillon. Yet the new dining room that opens on to an indoor garden is a big hit with the customers: there will always be a public for the luxurious establishments that we once thought were a dying breed.

Jean-Paul Bonin orchestrates the kitchen of Les Ambassadeurs, the Hôtel Crillon.

Lucas-Carton is another case in point. The restaurant was saved in the nick of time by the owner of Rémy Martin Cognac and Krug Champagne. Already well known in the previous century, around 1900 Lucas-Carton was a favourite with political personalities and financial wheeler-dealers, who downed epic meals in its Belle Epoque dining room (which is now a historical monument). Afterwards, those very grave messieurs would climb discreetly to the small private rooms on the upper floor, to tipple Champagne in far more amusing company.

It was over a luncheon at Lucas-Carton on November 10, 1918, that Foch, Joffre, Pershing, and French fixed the hour of the Armistice for the following day. Years later, Churchill often dropped in to sample the Lucas-Carton house specialty, woodcock with foie gras flamed in Cognac. After World War II, Lucas-Carton was still a great house. The chef in those days was a remarkable man named Mars Soustelle who had trained the then-obscure cooks named Paul Bocuse, Jean Troisgros, and Alain Senderens. In the 1960s Lucas-Carton was among the capital's foremost restaurants. The cream of Parisian society flocked to this address on the Place de la Madeleine. In his fabulously rich wine cellar, owner Alex Allegrier used to host extraordinary candlelight dinners for his friends, and serve such marvels as Romanée-Conti 1937 and Chartreuse 1900. After the death of chef Soustelle, the restaurant's cuisine went downhill. When the sale of Lucas-Carton was confirmed in early 1985, only a very few former patrons still frequented the dusty dining room.

The sale, in fact, had almost fallen through. When the Allegrier family learned that the buyer intended to establish Alain Senderens at Lucas-Carton, they vetoed the deal: it was unthinkable to them that a former employee should be master at Lucas-Carton! In the end, though, the sale went through. The renovation work was finished in a few months' time, and Senderens threw open the doors of an entirely restored restaurant, again one of the most beautiful in Paris: warm blond wood, comfortable banquette seating, seductively soft lighting, and the small first-floor salons in fresh new colours. The pleasure one feels at Senderens' table is unalloyed; the sense of well-being that comes of dining in handsome surroundings intensifies the delights of a cuisine that is surely one of today's most creative. Ironically, the moment Senderens took over and revived the kitchens at Lucas-Carton, the sophisticates who had rarely poked their elegant noses into his former restaurant (the small L'Archestrate on the Left Bank) clamoured for reservations at Senderens' new venue.

It is necessary to reserve a table at Lucas-Carton at least two weeks in advance. Neither of the two adjoining rooms has any particular advantage over the other; nor are there "good" or "bad" tables. Normally, it is Alain Senderens' wife, Eventhia, attractive, elegant, and just a bit shy, who welcomes diners at the door; but sometimes that duty devolves to the head waiter or even the cloakroom attendant. This occasional lapse in the quality of the reception is undeniably a weak point. However, the large and highly professional staff provides faultless service, devoid of needless ceremony or flourishes.

The food, with its bold, daring flavours, is not always understood by first-time diners, but the menu is catholic enough to suit most tastes. For example, for those who cannot stand "nouvelle cuisine," the menu offers one of the best ribs of beef to be found in Paris. Senderens garnishes it with wonderful deep-fried potato skins. But it would be a shame to neglect such delights as the millefeuille of duck liver with celery and apples, the bay scallop ravioli with courgettes, the lightly smoked poached salmon with asparagus, boned pigeon served with a ragoût of red peppers, spiny lobster with leeks, sweetbreads with wild mushrooms, or the canard Apicius (roasted duck with honey). Determined to make good food healthful as well, Senderens has banished sauces from his repertory, usually replacing them with cooking juices or vegetable-based liaisons. Although he hasn't managed to eliminate fat entirely, he never adds a single unnecessary gram to his dishes; hence the delicacy of his cuisine, which lets you rise from the table with a light stomach.

The wine cellar is exceedingly well stocked. In 1985, a customer from California shelled out $6,000 . . . just for the wine bill! His table of eight had ordered some of the greatest vintages of the century: Château d'Yquem 1947, Lafite-Rothschild 1945, and Petrus 1953.

Taillevent, located in a little street near the Champs-Elysées, cannot boast as long a history as Lucas-Carton, yet the restaurant is a monument nonetheless. Founded just after the last war by André Vrinat, Taillevent is located in a private mansion that once belonged to the Duc de Morny, half-brother of Napoleon III. (The restaurant's name recalls France's first chef, Guillaume Tirel, known as Taillevent. Besides serving as head cook from 1368 to 1371 to Charles VI, he compiled a cookbook, called *Le Viandier*.) For a while the restaurant was celebrated chiefly for the riches of its wine cellar: 130,000 bottles, including such collectors' items as a Romanée-Conti 1899, a Château d'Yquem 1869, and a Lafite-Rothschild 1806.

Taillevent would undoubtedly have aged just as sedately as Lasserre, a restaurant that appeared on the Parisian scene at about the same time, and suffered the same—relative—eclipse, had André Vrinat not turned the restaurant over to his son, Jean-Claude, in 1975. The latter infused new blood into the enterprise and quickly made it one of the finest restaurants in France. Jean-Claude Vrinat had no particular vocation for the restaurant business; in fact, he had no special knowledge of food. He had just graduated from the Institut des Hautes Etudes Commerciales (the French equivalent of the Harvard Business School) when his father asked

The luxurious Art Nouveau interior at Lucas-Carton in Paris was designed by Louis Majorelle.

32

him to come to work at Taillevent. Although he did not become a chef himself, Jean-Claude threw himself into his job with so great a passion that he totally transformed Taillevent's ultra-classic style. He sent chef Claude Deligne to training stints with the Troisgros brothers in Roanne (near Lyons), and with Fredy Girardet in Switzerland; today, Vrinat is still involved in the creation of every new dish served in his restaurant. Such professionalism explains the success of Taillevent, one of the rare great restaurants in France where the owner is not also the chef. A modest man—he considers Joël Robuchon's cuisine superior to that of his own restaurant—Vrinat pays painstaking attention to every detail; he surely merits the title "premier restaurateur of France."

Tables must be reserved several weeks in advance at Taillevent—especially for the evening. Tables are laid in three connecting rooms; never more than one hundred guests are served in a single evening so that service is impeccable. The decor is sober but very elegant, with carved paneling, old paintings, and lighting designed to be soft yet sufficient. The service is irreproachable, without a hint of servility. All in all dinner at Taillevent is a gala event. The cuisine, incidentally, is in constant progress. Less daring than Senderens' style, it is infinitely more inventive than what you would find at Lasserre—which for a long time many put on an equal footing with Taillevent. The Taillevent style is a "new classicism": witness such dishes as roast prawns with orange butter, red mullet with black olives, fish and seafood pot-au-feu, sweet-and-sour duck garnished with shredded potatoes and mushrooms, veal kidney with preserved shallots, salmis of pigeon with beef marrow, and the array of delicious desserts.

Each year at holiday time, accompanied by

Taillevent is in a Parisian mansion that once belonged to Napoleon III's half-brother.

his wife, Sabine, Jean-Claude tours the wine regions of France to hunt up new additions to a wine list that is far more than just a sequence of famous names. It is possible to come up with Bordeaux and Burgundies tariffed at around 100 francs that will steady your bill a bit. But if you decide to treat yourself to a really fine old Bordeaux of fifty years or more, you need only ask for it.

A handful of other Parisian restaurant landmarks deserve mention too: Lapérouse is still another example of an endangered monument that was saved in extremis. The food there is not exceptional, but certainly worthy enough to attract diners to its tiny dining rooms and low-ceilinged private salons, where Belle Epoque courtesans used to scratch their names on the mirrors with diamonds, while they supped with their rich protectors.

In the gardens of the Champs-Elysées, across from the presidential palace, two other century-old restaurants have recently been revived: Laurent, re-decorated at great cost by British millionaire Jimmy Goldsmith, is one of the best-known rendezvous places for political and business figures. A bit farther down the road is the Pavillon de l'Elysée, taken over and renovated by a property promoter who put the celebrated pastry chef Gaston Lenôtre in charge of the kitchens. No visit to Paris would be complete without a luncheon or dinner on the second floor of the Eiffel Tower, where not long ago a singularly beautiful luxury restaurant called the Jules Verne opened to great acclaim. It is proving to be an immense success: the food is top-notch and the view of the capital is thrilling.

In this instance, too, huge sums of money were needed to resurrect the historic site. It would seem that large companies are willing to risk investing in such ventures. Maybe someday we shall see the Elysée Palace converted into a restaurant! Stranger things have happened. Long before it became the French White House, the Elysée Palace belonged to Madame de Pompadour. It was confiscated during the French Revolution, and subsequently rented out to an Italian ice cream maker who served meals there!

34

The taste of well made quenelles is not quickly forgotten. In rouget à l'orientale, Alain Senderens prepares his with eggplant, red snapper, olive oil, and anchovies.

Alain Senderens

ROUGET A L'ORIENTALE

MEDITERRANEAN SNAPPER WITH OLIVE QUENELLES AND A VEGETABLE TART

VEGETABLE TART
150	g (5 oz) prepared puff pastry
1	small aubergine, thinly sliced
1	small courgette, thinly sliced
2	tomatoes, thinly sliced
30	ml (2 tbsp) olive oil
3.75	ml (¾ tsp) thyme

OLIVE QUENELLES:
	Salt
1	small aubergine, halved lengthways and scored with a sharp knife on cut surfaces
30	ml (2 tbsp) olive oil
1	piece of red snapper fillet, about 75 g (3 oz), skin removed
15	black olives, stoned
2	anchovy fillets

SNAPPER FILLETS AND VEGETABLE GARNISHES:
4	slices ripe tomato, 1 cm (½ inch) thick
	Salt and freshly ground pepper
	About 225 ml (8 fl oz) olive oil
225	g (8 oz) parsley leaves
30	ml (2 tbsp) unsalted butter
6	ripe tomatoes, peeled, seeded, and coarsely chopped
	Pinch of saffron threads, diluted in 15 ml (1 tbsp) hot water
15	g (½ oz) celery leaves
4	red snapper fillets, 175 g (6 oz) each, skin intact

Prepare vegetable tart: Heat oven to 200C (400F) gas 6. On a lightly floured surface, roll out puff pastry to a 25 x 15 cm (10 x 6 inch) rectangle; prick all over with a fork. Arrange aubergine, courgette and tomato slices on pastry in overlapping lengthways rows. Brush with olive oil and sprinkle with thyme. Refrigerate for 15 minutes.

Bake tart for about 25 minutes or until vegetables are tender and pastry is golden brown and crisp.

Prepare olive quenelles: Salt cut surfaces of aubergine halves and invert on a rack to drain for 30 minutes. Rinse aubergine and place on a baking sheet. Brush cut sides with 25 ml (1½ tbsp) olive oil

and bake for about 30 minutes or until tender. Remove aubergine from oven.

In a frying pan, heat remaining olive oil. Add fish fillet and sauté over medium-high heat for about 2 minutes or until it flakes when pierced with a knife. Transfer to a food processor. Scrape aubergine flesh from skins and add to processor with olives and anchovies; purée until blended and set aside.

Prepare snapper fillets and vegetable garnishes: Place tomato slices in a non-metallic ovenproof dish, season with salt and pepper, and cover with 100 ml (4 fl oz) olive oil. Bake for 12 minutes or until tender. Transfer tomato slices to kitchen towels to drain.

Blanch parsley in a large saucepan of boiling salted water for 2 minutes. Drain, wrap in a kitchen towel, and squeeze to extract all moisture. Place parsley in a food processor and purée with butter. Transfer to a small saucepan and season with salt and pepper to taste.

In a small saucepan, combine chopped tomatoes and saffron. Cook over medium-high heat, stirring frequently, for about 10 minutes or until most of the liquid has evaporated and the sauce is chunky. Season with salt and pepper and set aside.

Pour 1 cm (½ inch) olive oil into a frying pan and heat until almost smoking. Add celery leaves and fry for about 10 seconds or until crisped but not brown; drain on kitchen towels.

In a large pan, heat 45 ml (3 tbsp) olive oil. Season snapper fillets with salt and pepper and cut each into thirds on the diagonal. When oil is hot, add fish, skin side down, and sauté over medium-high heat, turning once, for about 9 minutes or until lightly browned and cooked through.

To serve: Re-heat quenelle mixture, parsley purée, tomato slices, and tomato sauce. Place a tomato slice topped with parsley purée in centre of each of 4 plates. With 2 spoons, shape olive mixture into ovals and place 3 around tomato on each plate. Place a fish fillet at top of quenelles, and top with a little tomato sauce and a few celery leaves. Cut tart into four lengthways strips and slice each strip into thirds. Place strips between olive quenelles and serve immediately.

Makes 4 servings

Ed. note: The original version of this recipe calls for rouget, a small Mediterranean fish.

Claude Deligne

SUPREMES DE VOLAILLE AU FOIE GRAS

CHICKEN BREASTS STUFFED WITH FOIE GRAS

30	ml (2 tbsp) unsalted butter
2.25	kg (5 lb) chicken pieces, chopped
1	large carrot, finely chopped
7	shallots, finely chopped
1	small onion, finely chopped
½	small celeriac, finely chopped
100	g (4 oz) mushrooms, finely chopped
1	clove garlic, finely chopped
100	ml (4 fl oz) dry vermouth
900	ml (1½ pints) rich chicken stock
1	bouquet garni
2	large chicken breasts, halved, boned, and skinned
150	g (5 oz) duck foie gras, cut into 8 slices
	Salt and freshly ground pepper
1	egg white
65	g (2½ oz) fresh bread crumbs (from 5 slices white bread, crusts removed)
100	ml (4 fl oz) crème fraîche
175	g (6 oz) unsalted butter, clarified

Heat oven to 230C (450F) gas 8.

In a large casserole, melt butter. Add chicken pieces and cook over medium heat, stirring for about 10 minutes or until very lightly browned. Add carrot, shallots, onion, celeriac, mushrooms, and garlic; stir well, and place in oven. Bake, stirring from time to time, for about 30 minutes or until carcasses and vegetables are nicely browned. Pour contents of casserole into a colander set over a bowl to drain.

Set casserole over medium-high heat and deglaze with vermouth; boil, scraping bottom of casserole with a wooden spoon, for about 3 minutes or until liquid is syrupy. Add stock and bouquet garni and stir well. Return drained carcasses and vegetables to casserole and bring to the boil over high heat. Reduce heat to medium and simmer, skimming as necessary, for 45 minutes.

Meanwhile, remove any large tendons from chicken breasts. Detach fillet from underside of each breast and set aside. With a sharp knife, cut a lengthways slit in each breast to form a pocket. Place 2 slices of foie gras in each pocket and press to seal; replace fillets to completely seal openings.

Bring water to the boil in a steamer. Season breasts with salt and pepper and place them in steamer, smooth side down. Cover and steam for 6 minutes; remove and pat dry. When breasts have cooled slightly, brush them with egg white and roll in bread crumbs to coat well. Set aside on a rack to dry for about 15 minutes.

Strain rich stock through a fine-mesh sieve set over a saucepan; press hard on bones and vegetables to extract all liquid. Add crème fraîche and bring to the boil over medium-high heat. Simmer sauce, skimming as necessary, for about 15 minutes or until reduced by half. (The sauce should be of a light-coating consistency.)

Just before serving, heat clarified butter in a medium frying pan. Add chicken breasts, in batches if necessary, and fry for 2 to 3 minutes on each side or until nicely browned. Drain on kitchen towels. Reheat sauce, if necessary. Spoon some of the sauce on to 4 plates and place a chicken breast half on each. Pass remaining sauce in sauce-boat.

Makes 4 servings

Ed. note: The original version of this recipe calls for Bresse chickens. If you can find large, free-range chickens, by all means use them. Remove the breasts for this dish, reserve the legs for another use, and use the carcasses for the sauce.

Chicken breasts stuffed with foie gras are served by Claude Deligne at Taillevent with a sauce prepared from, among other things, shallots, celeriac, mushrooms, dry vermouth, and rich chicken stock.

er, one will spend a memorable few hours.

With Alain Chapel, we truly enter the world of creative cuisine. Although he never wished to be linked with a particular school, this son of an ultraconservative innkeeping family from the countryside near Lyons unquestionably brought a new, personal tone to French cuisine. His chef friends and colleagues consider Chapel to be the most knowledgeable of them all. He transformed his unprepossessing little family inn, which stands by the roadside in the village of Mionnay, into an elegant establishment. With its indoor garden enclosed by an arcaded gallery, the place has a Provençal air about it that is unexpected in this land of ponds and swamps, peopled by myriad birds. In summer guests are seated in the cool of the gallery, in winter in the charming dining room with its pink stone floor and white stone fireplace. Flowers abound; the room is a jewel of elegant simplicity.

Alain Chapel is reserved, less a restaurateur than a chef; he does not glad-hand his guests, and his otherwise charming house lacks the harmony and feeling of comfort that one normally expects to find. The welcome is tepid, the service kind but not always very precise, and some have complained that the cooking is inconsistent. Could this complaint be due to the atmosphere?—guests are often as sensitive to the reception as they are to the cooking.

Guests are usually started off with an aperitif—pink Champagne, for example—in the garden or the little salon next to the dining room while they wait. There will probably be some delightful pre-dinner nibbles—tiny fried fish and fried parsley, a thyme- and pepper-scented aspic of young rabbit, or tuna with ginger. The menu and the fixed-price meals change so often it's impossible to have favourites, but let me describe my last meal at Alain Chapel's. There was a cream of clams and sea urchins; small red mullet served with coriander stems and tops heightened by a sauce with just a hint of mustard; a ragoût of Breton lobster garnished with marvellous minature red potatoes that were at once firm and tender; a casserole of small wild birds served with a risotto braised in the cooking juices; admirable goat cheeses, one fresh, one

ripened; and, finally, a fantastic bitter chocolate marquise. Chapel got the recipe from an old farmwoman, and he guards it as jealously as a family secret. The vanilla and cinnamon ice cream is like nothing to be found in a supermarket! The wine cellar is one of the richest in France, with a staggering (and costly) collection of Chambertins, Richebourgs, Hermitages, and Claret as well, for, even at the Burgundian border, people drink as much Claret as Burgundy. For all this, Chapel does not sell himself cheap; indeed, his is one of the most expensive restaurants in France.

Alain Chapel's place may give you the feeling of being in Provence, but, at Roger Vergé's place, not far from Cannes, you know you're really there. Nowadays all the celebrities who visit the Riviera stop off at this pretty, sun-drenched house, Le Moulin de Mougins, where the big mill wheel is still to be seen, just beside a delightful, closed garden surrounded by thick walls of greenery. "Except for the Pope," says Vergé, "I can't think of a single great name that hasn't passed through here." On summer evenings, he serves 150 meals (reserve a garden table), 90 percent of them to foreigners, among them Arab princes and Texas billionaires.

To describe the kind of cooking he does, Vergé uses the expressive phrase, "It's the cuisine of the sun." Its clarity, its free use of aromatic herbs and local vegetables, its light sauces and keen flavours, make it a typically Provençal cuisine with which Vergé mixes his own ideas, know-how, and very personal style. While he isn't a southerner himself (he comes from the centre of France) he has totally absorbed the spirit of Provence. Vergé is a true creator. Although the cooking of, say, Bocuse has had no influence on the younger generation of cooks, Vergé's "cuisine of the sun" has left its mark on many an up-and-coming chef.

Each year, about fifty new dishes are added to the list of favourite specialities like the violet artichokes à la barigoule (sautéed in olive oil and white wine); the gâteau of rabbit in Chablis; spiny lobster with pink peppercorns; lobster in Sauternes; fillet of bass with shallots and white Provençal wine; noisettes of lamb with truffle purée; or pigeon with garlic and chicory. Among recent and exciting discoveries at the Moulin are the sautéed Provençal vegetables with a wild mushroom purée; truffle-stuffed courgette blossoms; sage leaf fritters (the batter is so light it seems transparent); tiny red mullet with tomatoes and herb-scented olive oil; baked turbot sprinkled with chervil-flavoured oil; and the tender, pink fillet of veal with tomato purée. The entire array of desserts, which used to be a bit pale, is now superb.

Everyone wants to be on hand for dinner, so the waiting list is miles long during the height of the summer season. Yet at lunchtime there is plenty of room and a good time to reserve for those not afraid of feeling a little alone. The staff has more time, the kitchen is less rushed, their work is more consistent. At whatever time, it's going to cost. The wines are excellent and expensive. The Burgundies, however, command lower prices than do the Clarets; and for those who like a Provençal wine, the Château Vignelaure, the Château Simone, and the Château Pradeaux, a delicious red Bandol, are the best in the house.

Louis Outhier has transformed a tumbledown house in La Napoule, a little pleasure port near Cannes, into an opulent, even slightly ostentatious, restaurant, L'Oasis. The Louis XV decor seems somehow out of place in the light and atmosphere of the Riviera; try to reserve one of the few tables in the glassed-in gallery

The dessert table is an eye-catcher of Alain Chapel's restaurant. Chapel jealously guards the secret of his bitter chocolate marquise.

that borders the lovely indoor garden.

Along with Bocuse and the Troisgros brothers, Louis Outhier was one of Fernand Point's last pupils. A shy, nervous man, he was greatly influenced by Point early in his career, but his own style developed progressively. Back in the 1960s his specialties were bass in pastry (like Bocuse), truffle in puff pastry, and whole veal kidney in sherry. Outhier seemed to be getting into a rut until, a few years ago, his style underwent a dramatic change when he travelled to the Far East. The Hotel Oriental in Bangkok had invited him to supervise the cuisine prepared in their French restaurant, and there Outhier became fascinated with exotic spices and herbs. In a surprising turnabout, this ultraconservative cook was transformed into an enthusiastic creator.

Classics like his egg with caviar, his turbot braised in Champagne, hen with morels, John Dory in red wine, or strips of duck breast in Armagnac—excellent dishes, incidentally—are still on his menu. He is a master craftsman of this traditional sort of repertory, but it is in the other, more creative register that Outhier is a veritable artist. Ask for his prawn soup with Japanese tapioca, lemon thyme, and hot pepper; or the skate with truffles, lemon, and white wine vinegar; or perhaps his marvellous spiny lobster with Thai herbs (lemon grass, ginger, curry, and apples); the sliced lamb with ginger and broad beans; or the crusty duck Oriental, served with a sensational sauce that features honey, coriander, and Thai herbs. Outhier's cuisine may leave some palates bemused, but, to my mind, it is an experience not to be missed. Don't forget to save room for dessert. Gilles Falaschi, the Oasis pastry chef, is an artist in his own right, and it is nigh impossible to keep a cool head when confronted by his spectacular dessert trolley.

We began our visit to the founding fathers of nouvelle cuisine at Michel Guérard's beautiful house in the Landes, and we will end it there, for it has become an international symbol of French elegance and taste. This youthful man of fifty with the face of a choir boy is undoubtedly the most energetic, enthusiastic, and innovative member of the old association. The son of a butcher, Guérard has worked in kitchens since the age of seventeen. He soon rebelled against the humdrum routine that tied chefs down in those days. Like Vergé, he met Bocuse and the Troisgros brothers in 1962; the need for freedom that had long been gnawing him finally became irresistible. After the encounter he wrote in his diary: "From now on I'm going to cook the way the bird sings!" He started out in a dingy Parisian suburb where he ran a little bistro called the Pot-au-Feu. Despite the locale, it was clear that a great cook had just emerged on the scene.

Guérard had swift and phenomenal success with chic Parisians, who found it amusing to ride out to the capital's industrial waste lands for a meal. But soon afterwards, our young chef married; his wife, Christine, carried him off to the southwest of France, to Eugénie-les-Bains, a small, Napoleon III-era thermal spa, which the bride's father was attempting to revive. It seemed a risky venture, and Guérard's friends tried to dissuade him. Who would pay attention to fine cuisine in an out-of-the-way spot like that?

As it happened, Guérard's hunch was correct. When he opened in the month of March, he found he had a full house, with guests from all over the world. Miraculously, nothing could be less "touristy" than this spacious white house surrounded by woods and fields. The wrought-iron balconies that bring New Orleans to mind,

46

In summer the waiting list is miles long for Roger Vergé's Provençal cuisine at Le Moulin de Mougins on the Riviera.

the palm and banana trees that flourish in the mild climate of France's southwest, the Romantic paintings, the mahogany furniture, the Art Nouveau curios, the tables all festively laid, the bottles of aged Armagnac and pots of jam neatly aligned on shelves—every single detail is ravishing. A feeling of serenity and intimacy reigns at Michel Guérard, unexpected in a house where so many people come and go.

Those fortunate enough to visit the kitchens with Guérard will grasp the special spirit of the place. The team of fifteen men and women directed by chef Didier Oudil seem more like a group of friends than a typical kitchen brigade. A mood of co-operation reigns as they inspect the baskets of wild mushrooms gathered that morning, the foies gras fresh from their wrappers, the just-picked herbs still wet with dew. The illusion of improvisation ends when Guérard gets to work. Despite his occasionally dishevelled appearance, he is a born organizer. He puts each dish together with the precision of a chemist, particularly when it's one of his "light cuisine" specialties. Guérard's low-calorie cooking is the best of its type on earth. It allows those taking the slimming cure to shed several pounds in ten days while they indulge in crayfish, lobster, pigeon, and even rich-looking desserts. Low-calorie cuisine demands particularly painstaking attention from the chef, but Guérard's results are frankly amazing. Anyone spending a couple of days at Michel and Christine's inn should have at least one "light" meal (one thousand calories). Your tastebuds won't believe that it is diet food.

The majority of guests don't return to Eugénie-les-Bains to lose weight, but rather to enjoy what Guérard so prettily terms his "cuisine gourmande," food lover's food: it is ever-changing, as beautiful to behold as it is heavenly to eat. Every one of his creations is captivating, whether it is the fresh foie gras with pepper; the little truffle- or morel-stuffed ravioli; the whole roasted lobster smoked right in the fireplace; the salmon served with lemon-flavoured crayfish fritters; skate roasted in bacon slices with a sauce that includes Graves wine and lobster coral; the daube of local duck and pig's trotters, the pigeon with cabbage; the farm-raised chicken with parsley; or any of the divine desserts: from the thin, hot apple tart (often imitated, never equalled) to the cornucopia of glacéed fruit.

Michel Guérard's brand of cooking is the epitome of anti-"grande cuisine." There is a pinch of genius in these dishes, too, in the transformation of simple, direct, rustic flavours by a seemingly inexhaustible imagination. But watch out: Eugénie-les-Bains casts a bewitching spell; people have been known to go one day for lunch and, two days later, find themselves still there.

Cerfeuil

Michel Guérard's cuisine owes its flavour to the fresh herbs he harvests daily. Facing page: Christine and Michel Guérard.

SAUMON OU LOUP EN CROUTE
FERNAND POINT, SAUCE CHORON

SALMON OR STRIPED BASS
IN PASTRY WITH
CHORON SAUCE

SALMON

15	ml	(1 tbsp) olive oil
1.25		-1.5 kg (2½-3 lb) salmon or striped bass fillets from whole fish, skin removed and central bone detached, but reserved, optional
15	ml	(1 tbsp) finely chopped parsley
15	ml	(1 tbsp) finely chopped chervil
10	ml	(2 tsp) finely chopped tarragon
		Salt and freshly ground pepper to taste
225	g	-350 g (8-12 oz) puff pastry, fresh or frozen
15	ml	(1 tbsp) unsalted butter
1		egg yolk

SIMPLIFIED CHORON SAUCE:

50	ml	(2 fl oz) wine vinegar
30	ml	(2 tbsp) finely chopped shallots
30	ml	(2 tbsp) finely chopped tarragon
		Salt and freshly ground pepper to taste
2		egg yolks
50	ml	(2 tbsp) water
100	g	(4 oz) plus 30 ml (2 tbsp) cold butter, cut into pieces
		Juice of 1 lemon
5	ml	(1 tsp) tomato purée
15	ml	(1 tbsp) finely chopped chervil

50

Prepare fish: Brush a large plate with oil and place fish on it. Sprinkle herbs on both sides of each fillet; season with salt and pepper to taste.

Butter an ovenproof dish large enough to hold fish and line with a piece of buttered greaseproof paper of the same size.

On a floured surface, evenly roll pastry into 2 rectangles the size of the fish. Place one rectangle in the prepared dish and lay fish on top of it. With a brush dipped in water, moisten edges of pastry. Place second layer of pastry on top of fish. Cut pastry around fillets to form a fish shape, making a head, tail, and fins. Lightly press edges of pastry to seal. With the wide end of a small metal piping nozzle, make impressions on pastry to resemble fish scales. Use trimmings to decorate fish with an eye, gills, and fins. Brush yolk over fish to glaze.

Bake fish in preheated oven for about 15 minutes, reduce temperature to 180C (350F) gas 4, and continue to bake for another 20 to 30 minutes (cooking time will depend on thickness of fish).

Prepare sauce: In a small, heavy enamel saucepan, combine vinegar, shallots, 15 ml (1 tbsp) tarragon, and salt and pepper to taste. Bring to the boil over medium heat and reduce until shallots and tarragon are wet, but liquid has evaporated. Remove from heat and cool. Add egg yolks and water to saucepan or transfer to double boiler and cook, whisking constantly, over very low heat. (Have heated sauce-boat on hand, as sauce will not keep.) Whisk in butter, lemon juice, and tomato purée and continue whisking for about 5 minutes or until sauce is light and thickened. Season to taste and add chervil and remaining tarragon. Keep sauce warm.

To serve: When fish is cooked, lift pastry crust at one end with a sharp knife; lift top fillet with a palette knife and remove central bone. Place fish on serving platter, replace top crust, and serve with choron sauce.

Makes 6 servings

Paul Bocuse first wraps salmon or striped bass in a pastry crust, bakes it, and serves it with choron sauce.

Paul Bocuse

VOLAILLE DE BRESSE HALLOWEEN

CHICKEN AND RICE COOKED IN A PUMPKIN WITH A PUMPKIN GRATIN

3.5	-4 kg (8-9 lb) round pumpkin, washed and dried
2	kg (4½ lb) free-range chicken, at room temperature
	Salt and freshly ground pepper
1	bunch fresh tarragon
10	sprigs parsley
75	g (3 oz) unsalted butter
175	g (6 oz) rice
475	ml (16 fl oz) water
2	eggs, beaten with 225 ml (8 fl oz) double cream
	Freshly grated nutmeg
50	g (2 oz) Gruyère cheese, grated

Heat oven to 200C (400F) gas 6.

Cut a hat, about 10 cm (4 inches) from top of pumpkin; remove and set aside. With a large, sturdy spoon, scoop out pumpkin seeds and discard. Scoop out pumpkin flesh, leaving a 1 cm (½ inch) shell; reserve flesh. Cover pumpkin shell with aluminium foil and place on a baking sheet.

Season cavity of chicken with salt and pepper and stuff with tarragon, parsley, and 50 g (2 oz) butter

Truss chicken and place it in pumpkin, breast side up. Replace hat on pumpkin, cover with aluminium foil, and bake for 2 hours. Soak rice in water.

Meanwhile, cook reserved pumpkin flesh in boiling salted water for 10 minutes. Drain well and transfer to an ovenproof casserole. Bake in heated oven, stirring from time to time, for about 40 minutes or until pumpkin is quite dry. (This can also be done on top of the oven.)

Whisk egg-cream mixture into pumpkin. (For a smoother mixture, purée pumpkin in a food processor with egg-cream mixture.) Season with salt and pepper to taste. Butter a medium gratin dish with remaining butter, add pumpkin mixture, and sprinkle with nutmeg and grated cheese.

Remove chicken from pumpkin. Drain rice and add to pumpkin, then replace chicken and the "hat." Bake chicken for about 1 hour or until the juices run clear when the thigh is pierced with a skewer and the rice is tender.

About 20 minutes before chicken is done, place pumpkin gratin in oven and bake until cheese is melted and mixture is heated through.

To serve: Remove chicken from pumpkin and discard trussing strings. Carve chicken into serving pieces. With a large spoon, scoop rice into a serving bowl. Serve chicken immediately, accompanied by rice and pumpkin gratin.

Makes 6 to 8 servings

Volaille de Bresse Halloween was made with American traditions in mind.

Pierre and Michel Troisgros
BRILLANT AU CARAMEL
CHOCOLATE CARAMEL TART

200	g (7 oz) sweet pie pastry
350	ml (12 fl oz) double cream
90	g (3½ oz) plain chocolate, melted
175	g (6 oz) sugar
15	ml (1 tbsp) plus 5 ml (1 tsp) golden syrup
45	ml (3 tbsp) water
7.5	ml (1½ tsp) fresh lemon juice

Heat oven to 180C (350F) gas 4. On a lightly floured surface, roll out pastry to a 23 cm (9 inch) round. Place on a heavy baking sheet and bake for about 14 minutes or until golden brown. Transfer to a rack to cool.

In a small saucepan, scald 100 ml (4 fl oz) cream over medium-high heat. Remove from heat and stir in melted chocolate. Set aside to cool, stirring occasionally, until mixture is just firm enough to hold its shape.

Spread a thin layer of chocolate mixture over pastry round. Scrape remaining chocolate mixture into a round bag fitted with a medium star piping nozzle. Pipe chocolate around rim of pastry to form a border; then, starting at centre of pastry, pipe the outline of 8 pie wedges. Refrigerate for about 30 minutes or until firm.

Meanwhile, make the caramel. In a heavy saucepan, combine sugar, golden syrup, and water. Bring to the boil over medium heat and cook for about 12 minutes or until lightly golden. Remove from heat and stir in remaining cream. (The mixture may sputter, so watch carefully.) Bring caramel to the boil over medium-high heat, stirring constantly. Remove from heat and stir in lemon juice. Let caramel cool to room temperature.

When caramel is cool, spoon it into the 8 outlined pie sections. Refrigerate tart for 30 minutes before serving, if desired.

Makes 8 servings

Brillant au Caramel, at the left, is one of Pierre and Michel Troisgros' tempting desserts.

Paul, Jean-Pierre,
and Marc Haeberlin

MOUSSELINE DE GRENOUILLES

FROG MOUSSELINES WITH SPINACH

100	g (4 oz) plus 30 ml (2 tbsp) unsalted butter
4	shallots, finely chopped
2	kg (4½ lb) fresh frogs' legs
375	ml (13 fl oz) Alsatian Riesling
	Salt and freshly ground pepper
225	g (8 oz) pike or perch fillets
2	egg whites
750	ml (1¼ pints double cream, well chilled
450	g (1 lb) fresh spinach leaves, washed and large stalks removed
1	clove garlic, unskinned
7.5	ml (½ tbsp) unsalted butter blended with 7.5 ml (½ tbsp) flour
	Fresh lemon juice
	Snipped fresh chives

Place bowl and steel blade of a food processor in freezer until thoroughly chilled.

In a large sauté pan, melt 25 ml (1½ tbsp) butter. Add shallots and sauté over medium-high heat, stirring constantly, for about 3 minutes or until translucent. Add half the frogs' legs, wine, and a pinch of salt and pepper. Bring to a simmer, stir well, and cover; cook, stirring from time to time, for 10 minutes.

Remove frogs' legs from the pan and set aside. Strain cooking liquid through a fine-mesh sieve set over a medium saucepan. Bring liquid to the boil and cook over medium-high heat, skimming as necessary, for about 9 minutes or until reduced by half.

Bone remaining raw frogs' legs. Remove bowl and blade from freezer, add fish fillets and frog meat, and purée. With machine running, gradually add egg whites; when whites are fully incorporated, gradually add 475 ml (16 fl oz) cream. Scrape mousseline into a medium bowl and blend in 3.75 ml (¾ tsp) salt and 8 grindings of fresh pepper. Refrigerate.

Bone cooked frogs' legs. Heat oven to 170C (325F) gas 3.

(Recipe continued on following page.)

Mousseline de grenouilles is a delicate speciality of the Haeberlins

Butter ten 150 g (5 oz) ramekins. Scrape mousseline into a piping bag fitted with a round nozzle. Pipe mixture into ramekins to generously cover bottoms and sides, and fill centres with some of the cooked frog meat. Cover and fill in with remaining mousseline; smooth surfaces with a palette knife. Place filled ramekins in a bain marie, cover with greaseproof paper, and bake for 15 to 19 minutes or until firm.

Meanwhile, blanch spinach leaves in boiling, salted water for 1 minute; drain well. In a frying pan, melt 30 ml (2 tbsp) butter with garlic. When butter foams, add spinach and cook over medium heat, tossing gently, for about 2 minutes or until heated through. Cover and keep warm.

Bring reduced cooking liquid to the boil over medium-high heat. Whisk in butter-flour mixture, a little at a time, and bring to the boil. Add remaining cream and return to the boil, whisking constantly. Remove from heat and whisk in remaining 97.5 ml (6½ tbsp) butter, 15 ml (1 tbsp) at a time. Season to taste with salt and pepper, and lemon juice. Add remaining cooked frog meat to sauce and re-heat.

Spoon some sauce on to each plate and arrange spinach in centre. Unmould mousselines, draining if necessary, and place over spinach. Top with remaining sauce and sprinkle each serving with chives.
Makes 10 servings

Pierre and Michel Troisgros

MIXED BOEUF

FIVE CUTS OF BEEF WITH RED WINE AND SHALLOTS

225	ml (8 fl oz) dry red wine
3	shallots, thickly sliced
	Pinch of sugar
	Salt and freshly ground pepper
75	ml (5 tbsp) unsalted butter
225	g (8 oz) beef tenderloin cut 3 cm (1¼ inches) thick
225	g (8 oz) boneless rib steak, cut 1 cm (½ inch) thick
175	g (6 oz) rump steak, cut into 4 slices
200	g (7 oz) boneless sirloin steak, cut into 4 slices
175	g (6 oz) skirt steak, cut into 4 slices

The Troisgros dish of five cuts of beef can be prepared easily and quickly.

In a small saucepan, combine wine and shallots with a pinch each of sugar and salt; bring to the boil and set aside.

Season meats with salt and pepper. In both a small and medium frying pan melt 25 ml (1½ tbsp) butter over medium-high heat. When butter begins to foam, add tenderloin to the small frying pan and rib steak to the medium pan. Cook tenderloin for 8 minutes, turning once; cook rib steak for 5 minutes, turning once. Remove meats from the frying pans and set meats and pans aside.

In a large frying pan, heat remaining 30 ml (2 tbsp) butter until foaming. Add sirloin, rump steak and skirt steak slices, in batches if necessary, and cook over medium-high heat, turning once, for 2 to 4 minutes (depending on thickness of meat). Remove meat from pan and divide evenly among 4 heated plates.

Cut both tenderloin and rib steak into 4 slices and place on plates.

Discard fat from all 3 frying pans and set them over high heat. Deglaze pans with shallot-wine mixture; season with salt and pepper to taste and pour this sauce over meats. Serve immediately.

Makes 4 servings

Ed. note: The French like their meat rare; if you prefer yours better done, add a few minutes to the cooking times given here.

Alain Chapel

TRANCHE DE BAR ROTI, SALSIFIS ET CREVETTES GRISES AU THYM CITRON, UNE SAUCE ACIDULEE

ROASTED SEA BASS WITH SALSIFY AND SHRIMP

52.5	ml (3½ tbsp) olive oil
2	carrots, finely chopped
1	onion, finely chopped
1	leek, well washed and finely chopped
2	sticks of celery, finely chopped
4	lobster carcasses, cut into pieces
15	ml (1 tbsp) Cognac
475	ml (16 fl oz) dry white wine
475	ml (16 fl oz) water
1	small head garlic
2	ripe tomatoes, quarted
8	sprigs parsley
	Salt
	Pinch of coarsely crushed black peppercorns
30	ml (2 tbsp) lemon juice
175	g (6 oz) plus 25 ml (1½ tbsp) flour
500	g (1¼ lb) salsify
5	sprigs lemon thyme
45	ml (3 tbsp) Italian balsamic vinegar
2	sea bass, about 750 g (1½ lb), head and tail removed, dressed, and halved crossways
	Freshly ground pepper
75	g (3 oz) cold unsalted butter
225	g (8 oz) cooked baby shrimp, peeled

In a large stockpot, heat 30 ml (2 tbsp) olive oil. Add carrots, onion, leek, celery, and lobster shells and cook over medium heat, stirring constantly, for about 7 minutes or until vegetables are soft and fragrant. Deglaze briefly with Cognac. Add wine, water, garlic, tomatoes, parsley, a pinch of salt and crushed peppercorns. Stir well and bring to the boil. Reduce heat and simmer for 1 hour.

Meanwhile, in a medium saucepan of salted water, combine lemon juice and 25 ml (1½ tbsp) flour. Peel salsify and rinse well under cold water. Slice salsify on the diagonal and drop slices into saucepan as you cut them. Bring to the boil over medium-high heat.

Reduce heat and simmer for about 12 minutes or until salsify is just tender. Drain in a colander under cold water and set aside.

Strain simmered stock through a fine-mesh sieve set over a saucepan, pressing hard on the solids to extract as much liquid as possible. Boil stock over high heat, skimming as necessary, for about 35 minutes or until reduced to 225 ml (8 fl oz). Add 1 sprig thyme and set aside to infuse for 5 minutes. Discard thyme and add balsamic vinegar; set aside.

Heat oven to 190C (375F) gas 5. Rinse bass under cold water and pat dry with kitchen towels. Brush with remaining olive oil and season on both sides with salt and pepper. Flour bass lightly, dusting off any excess. Place bass in a lightly oiled earthenware ovenproof dish and roast in the oven, turning once, for about 20 minutes or until the fish is nicely browned and just flakes when pierced with a knife.

Meanwhile, melt 30 ml (2 tbsp) butter in a large frying pan. Add salsify and sauté over medium-high heat, tossing frequently, for about 5 minutes or until lightly browned. Add shrimp.

To serve: Bring sauce to the boil over high heat. Remove from heat and whisk in remaining butter, 15 ml (1 tbsp) at a time. Re-heat salsify and shrimp for about 2 minutes or until warmed through. Pour sauce on to 4 plates and top with roasted bass. Surround fish with salsify and shrimp and garnish each serving with a sprig of lemon thyme.

Makes 4 servings

Alain Chapel

SAINT-PIERRE AU PLAT ET AU FOUR, COMME UNE SURPRISE

JOHN DORY FILLETS BAKED AS "SURPRISE"

FISH FUMET:

15	ml (1 tbsp) unsalted butter
15	ml (1 tbsp) chopped shallots
50	g (2 oz) chopped carrots
50	g (2 oz) chopped onions
	Bones from 2 whole John Dory, washed, drained, and roughly chopped
600	ml (1 pint) cold water

The "surprise" of Alain Chapel's John Dory fillets comes from baking them on a bed of onions for a couple of minutes.

JOHN DORY FILLETS:

2	whole John Dory 750 g-1 kg (1½ 2 lb) each, cut into fillets, or substitute sole
105	ml (7 tbsp) unsalted butter
	Salt and freshly ground pepper
16	small, firm, new potatoes, peeled and sliced 0.5 cm (¼ inch) thick
350	ml (12 fl oz) delicate chicken stock, hot, plus 50 ml (2 fl oz) chicken stock, warmed
12	to 16 spring onion tops, chopped
4	sprigs fresh thyme or lemon thyme
8	small sprigs fresh basil

Prepare fish fumet: In a heavy enamel or stainless-steel saucepan, melt butter. Add shallots, carrots, and onions and cook until soft, but not browned. Add fish bones and continue to cook for 3 to 5 minutes. Cover with cold water and simmer, skimming surface occasionally, for 20 minutes. Strain and return to a clean, heavy saucepan; cook until reduced to about 100 ml (4 fl oz).

Prepare John Dory fillets: Heat oven to 230C (450F) gas 8. Wash fish fillets and pat dry with kitchen towels; reserve in a clean cloth and refrigerate.

Using 15 ml (1 tbsp) butter for each, grease 4 small gratin dishes; add salt and pepper to taste. Decoratively arrange thin layers of potatoes (3 layers at most) on bottom of each dish. Moisten with 350 ml (12 fl oz) hot chicken stock and bake in the oven for about 10 minutes or until potatoes are just cooked, but still firm. In a heavy saucepan, melt 15 ml (1 tbsp) butter. Add spring onion tops and cook over low heat until onions are softened, but still firm. Remove potatoes from oven and arrange onions in a thin layer in centre of each dish.

In a heavy frying pan, melt remaining butter. Add fish and sauté over low to medium heat for about 3 minutes on each side or until fish is cooked, but still firm. Place fillets over onions in each dish and baste with a little butter from pan. Garnish with thyme and basil, and moisten with 45 ml (3 tbsp) fish fumet, remaining chicken stock, and some liquid from potatoes. Return to oven and cook for 1 to 2 minutes; serve immediately.

Makes 4 servings

LE BLANC DE TURBOT EN MOUSSELINE DE COING

WHITE OF TURBOT IN QUINCE MOUSSELINE

3 to 4 large, very ripe quinces, peeled, halved, and cored
100 ml (4 fl oz) water
Salt and freshly ground pepper
30 ml (2 tbsp) unsalted butter plus 30 ml (2 tbsp) butter, clarified
1.25 kg (2¼ lb) turbot, skinned, boned, and cut into 6 thin fillets, or substitute other firm fish
6 young, tender bay leaves, trimmed with sewing scissors
475 -750 ml (16 fl oz-1¼ pints) double cream
10 ml (2 tsp) chopped fresh parsley leaves
10 ml (2 tsp) chopped fresh chervil leaves
10 fresh tarragon leaves

Heat oven to 190C (375F) gas 5. With a sharp knife, cut quinces into 24 very thin slices. Chop remaining quinces. In a heavy saucepan, combine chopped quinces, water and a pinch of salt. Cook until soft. Transfer mixture to a food processor, add 30 ml (2 tbsp) butter, and purée (you should have about 750 ml (1¼ pints). Set aside and reserve.

In a large ovenproof dish, arrange fish fillets. Place 4 quince slices and a bay leaf on each fillet and salt to taste. Add enough double cream to cover fish and bake in the oven for about 8 minutes or until fish is very white.

Remove from oven and strain cooking liquid into a small, heavy saucepan; leave just enough liquid in dish to keep fish from becoming dry; cover with aluminium foil and keep warm.

Bring cream to the boil and, whisking constantly, add 50 ml (2 fl oz) quince purée. Remove from heat and place in blender with parsley, chervil, and tarragon. Blend until sauce becomes velvety and light green in colour. Keep warm.

To serve: Spoon a thin layer of quince purée and

a thin layer of herb sauce to cover the bottom of 6 warmed plates. Place a fish fillet on each plate. With a brush dipped in melted butter, brush surface of fish to remove all traces of cream.

Makes 6 servings

Ed. Note: To give fish a nice white colour, place fillets in a large bowl and cover completely with 900 ml (1½ pints) cold milk, a few ice cubes, and a little water, if necessary. Refrigerate for at least 2 hours; strain just before cooking.

Roger Vergé

LES FLEURS DE COURGETTE AUX TRUFFES

COURGETTE FLOWERS STUFFED WITH WHOLE TRUFFLES

50	g (2 oz) unsalted butter, plus 225 g (8 oz) cold butter, cut into pieces
15	ml (1 tbsp) finely chopped shallot
450	g (1 lb) very white mushrooms, rinsed, dried, finely chopped, and sprinkled with 15 ml (1 tbsp) fresh lemon juice Salt and freshly ground pepper
50	ml (2 fl oz) plus 15 ml (1 tbsp) double cream
2	egg yolks
6	tiny courgettes, flowers attached, or substitute pumpkin flowers with pistils removed, blanched seakale, or green cabbage leaves
6	fresh black Vaucluse truffles (5 g (½ oz) each), or substitute preserved truffles and reserve juice
450	g (1 lb) young, tender spinach or Lamb's lettuce, washed and thick stems removed Fresh chervil leaves, to garnish

In a heavy saucepan, melt 60 ml (4 tbsp) butter over medium heat. Add shallots, mushrooms, and salt to taste. Cook, mixing with a wooden spoon, for 3 to 4 minutes. Strain mushrooms through a stainless mesh sieve or muslin; reserve liquid. Return mushrooms to saucepan and cook over medium to high heat for about 3 minutes or until they lose their moisture. Remove from heat and reserve.

In a mixing bowl, whisk together double cream and egg yolks. Pour over mushrooms and mix well. Place mixture in a small saucepan and cook over low heat for about 2 minutes; season to taste and spoon into a bowl to cool.

Gently open petals of courgette flowers, spread a little mushroom mixture inside, and place a truffle in the middle of each flower. (Or spread mushroom mixture on blanched seakale or cabbage leaves, top with truffles, and wrap into small parcels.) Place courgette on a small rack and reserve.

In a small, heavy saucepan, combine reserved mushroom juice and any truffle juice. Reduce over medium to high heat until only 45 ml (3 tbsp) liquid remain. Over medium heat, whisk in cold butter, 30 ml (2 tbsp) at a time, and add salt and pepper to taste; reserve and keep warm.

Steam filled courgettes for about 15 minutes or until tender.

To serve: Divide spinach or lamb's lettuce among 6 plates and arrange courgette on top. Coat with a little reserved mushroom-truffle sauce and garnish with chervil leaves, if desired.

Makes 6 servings

Roger Vergé's turbot fillets are baked with quince slices and a bay leaf in double cream.

Overleaf: Roger Vergé fills the courgette blossom— still attached to the courgette—with chopped mushrooms and truffles.

Roger Vergé

LE FILET DE CHEVREUIL, SAUCE POIVRADE FRAMBOISEE

FILLET OF VENISON WITH RED WINE AND RASPBERRIES

45	ml (3 tbsp) olive oil
1	onion, finely chopped
2	carrots, finely chopped
1	stick celery, finely chopped
4	cloves garlic, finely chopped
200	ml (4 fl oz) red wine vinegar
1	bottle Côte-Rôtie, Pommard, or Bandol
1	large bouquet garni made with 2 bay leaves, 1 bunch thyme, and 1 bunch parsley stems, tied with string
30	ml (2 tbsp) coarsely crushed black peppercorns
8	juniper berries
1	kg (2¼ lb) lean venison fillet
5	ml (1 tsp) tomato purèe
225	g (8 oz) fresh raspberries

25	ml (1½ tbsp) cornflour
100	g (4 oz) plus 15 ml (1 tbsp) unsalted butter
	Salt and freshly ground pepper
5	ml (1 tsp) redcurrant jelly
30	ml (2 tbsp) double cream

Heat olive oil in a large casserole. Add the onion, carrots, celery, and garlic and cook over medium heat, stirring frequently for about 15 minutes or until vegetables begin to brown. Add vinegar and bring to the boil over high heat; simmer for about 3 minutes or until liquid reduces to 15 ml (1 tbsp). Add wine, bouquet garni, pepper, and juniper berries and return to the boil. Simmer over medium heat for 20 minutes. Remove from heat and let marinade cool completely. (You can transfer marinade to another casserole to speed up cooling.)

Set venison fillet on a rack and place rack in casserole with marinade. Marinate, turning the meat from time to time, for 6 to 8 hours in a cool place, or overnight in the regrigerator. (If meat is refrigerated, bring it to room temperature before roasting.)

Remove venison from marinade and dry well with paper towels. Add tomato purée to marinade and cook over medium-high heat for about 8 minutes or until liquid reduces to 225 ml (8 fl oz); set marinade aside.

Preheat oven to 220C (425F) gas 7. Purée half the raspberries through a fine-mesh strainer. In a small bowl, combine cornflour with enough wine or water to form a thin paste.

Set a roasting pan over medium-high heat and add 30 ml (2 tbsp) butter. Season venison with salt and pepper. When butter stops foaming, add meat and sear for about 2 minutes, just until browned on all sides. Transfer venison to oven and roast for 15 to 20 minutes or until quite rare. (At 15 minutes, venison will be very rare; at 20 it will be rare to medium. If you prefer it better done, roast longer. Keep in mind that the meat will continue to cook after it is removed from the oven.) Remove meat from roasting pan, cover with aluminum foil, and set aside.

Meanwhile, prepare sauce. Drain fat from roasting pan and add reserved marinade. Set pan over medium heat and stir with a wooden spoon, scraping bottom to dislodge and dissolve any roasting juices. Strain mixture through a fine mesh strainer set over a medium saucepan; press hard on the solids to extract all juices. Stir in raspberry purée.

Set saucepan over medium heat and whisk in liquefied cornflour, a little at a time, until sauce is of desired consistency. (You may not need to use all the cornflour.) Whisk in remaining butter, 15 ml (1 tbsp) at a time. Stir in redcurrant jelly and season with salt and pepper to taste. In a small bowl, combine 50 ml (2 fl oz) sauce and double cream.

To serve: Slice meat and arrange on 6 heated plates. Grind fresh pepper over meat and ladle some sauce over each serving. Top with a little cream sauce and, with a fork, marble the two sauces together. Garnish with remaining raspberries. Pass remaining sauce in sauceboat.

Makes 6 servings

Ed. note: The chef serves this dish with chestnut purée and small pears poached in red wine.

Chef's Note: Many people enjoy the sauces that accompany game dishes but are not too fond of the meat itself; such is the case with me. The sauce for this dish could be used with any other good cut of venison, as well as with a beef fillet or a leg of lamb. If fresh raspberries are unavailable, as they often are during game season, you can use flash-frozen raspberries instead.

Louis Outhier

LANGOUSTES AUX HERBES THAI
ROCK LOBSTER WITH THAI HERBS

2	rock lobsters (1 kg (2 lb) each), or substitute lobsters
30	ml (2 tbsp) unsalted butter
5	ml (1 tsp) dried green and red hot peppers or peppery curry powder
2	leaves lemon grass, cut into thin strips
5	ml (1 tsp) minced shallots
30	ml (2 tbsp) grated fresh root ginger
2	carrots, peeled, cut into long, thin strips, or grated
2	Golden Delicious apples, cut into long, thin strips
175	ml (6 fl oz) white port
2.5	ml (½ tsp) turmeric
225	ml (8 fl oz) double cream, whipped
	Salt to taste

(Recipe continued on following page.)

71

Preceding pages: Louis Outhier discovered Asian seasoning when he visited the East; one result is his lobster with Thai herbs.

Left: Fillet of venison with red wine and raspberries is another Vergé creation.

Michel Guérard

LES ECREVISSES CUITES A L'ETOUFFEE EN MARINIERE DE LEGUMES

SMOTHERED CRAYFISH WITH BABY VEGETABLES

4	small potatoes
8	cloves garlic, unskinned, plus 1 clove garlic, skinned and finely chopped
4	shallots, unskinned
	Salt
	Sugar
4	baby carrots with tops
4	baby turnips with tops
4	spring onions with tops
4	small leeks, well washed
1.75	kg (4 lb) fresh mussels, scrubbed and de-bearded
50	ml (2 fl oz) dry white wine
2.5	kg (5½ lb) live crayfish, well rinsed
	Bouquet garni
6	large fresh basil leaves
15	ml (1 tbsp) olive oil
90	g (3½ oz) unsalted butter
	Freshly ground pepper
15	ml (1 tbsp) finely chopped parsley
	Fresh chervil leaves

78

In a medium saucepan, combine potatoes, unskinned garlic cloves, and shallots. Cover with cold water, salt lightly, and bring to the boil over high heat. Reduce heat to medium and cook for about 15 minutes or until potatoes are barely tender. Drain, discard garlic and shallots, and set aside.

In a saucepan of salted, lightly sugared water, combine carrots, turnips, and onions. Bring to the boil and cook over medium-high heat for about 10 minutes or until vegetables are barely tender. Drain and refresh under cold water.

Cook leeks in boiling salted water for about 4 minutes or until just tender.

Place mussels in a large saucepan. Cover and cook over high heat, shaking pan occasionally, for about 7 minutes or until mussels open. Transfer mussels to a bowl and reserve for another use. Strain cooking liquid and reserve (you should have about 475 ml (16 fl oz)).

In a large, heavy casserole, arrange all cooked vegetables. Moisten with mussel liquid and wine and bring to the boil. Add crayfish and bouquet garni, cover, and cook over medium-high heat for 5 minutes. Set aside and let steam for 2 minutes longer.

Meanwhile, purée basil leaves and olive oil in a food processor.

To serve: Remove crayfish and arrange on 4 large plates. With a slotted spoon, remove vegetables from casserole and place one of each on each plate.

Add basil purée and chopped garlic to casserole and bring to the boil over high heat. Cook for about 10 minutes or until liquid is reduced to 300 ml (½ pint). Remove from heat and whisk in butter, 15 ml (1 tbsp) at a time. Season with salt and pepper to taste and strain through a fine-mesh sieve. Stir in parsley and spoon some sauce over each serving. Sprinkle with chervil and serve immediately.

Makes 4 servings

Crayfish and baby vegetables are combined colourfully by Michel Guérard.

TODAY'S INNOVATORS

SINCE THE ARRIVAL OF BOCUSE, Troisgros, and the other founding fathers of modern cuisine, a new generation of chefs now in their late twenties and early thirties is quickly growing up behind them, impatient for a turn in the limelight. This explosion of culinary talent burst forth four or five years ago, and it gives no sign of losing momentum.

These men and (occasionally) women are the innovators of today. Having learned from the successes as well as the failures of their nouvelle cuisine predecessors, they have discovered a balance that includes both past and present. They reject the worst of the modern school's eccentricities, without falling back on the grande cuisine of yesteryear. Their inspiration comes partly from the repertory of regional specialties, which they lighten and modernize, but, above all, they explore, they invent, they create. Some of these cooks have not only caught up with the elders of their craft: they have also outstripped many of them in terms of celebrity and sheer talent.

Obviously, not all are on the same level. Some have reached master status, like Alain Senderens, Joël Robuchon, Jacques Maximin, and Marc Meneau. Others, like Michel and Jean-Michel Lorain, Jean Bardet, Bernard Loiseau, Pierre Gagnaire, Michel Bras, Guy Savoy, or Alain Dutournier, are fast approaching that rank. Still others are moving forwards rapidly. The forty chefs discussed on the following tour are absolutely the crème de la crème.

In France, everything starts in Paris, and so shall we. Alain Senderens, the chef at Lucas-Carton, has already been mentioned. He is gaining a reputation world-wide for his superb cuisine. The young chef from south-western France began his successful career in a small Left Bank restaurant and has become one of the uncontested masters of French cuisine. His mind fairly teems with ideas, and despite the rare error or lapse, his talent has something of the genius about it. Like Michel Guérard, his name will go down in gastronomic history.

Joël Robuchon is also unquestionably one of the foremost culinary talents of France, indeed, of the world. His charming digs, with their elegant Old World flavour and pink and flowered chintz, are very popular. Reserving a table for dinner there is more difficult than speaking with the President.

Robuchon still has the rustic tastes and the respect for fine ingredients and pure flavours that come from his country childhood, yet he is first and foremost a dazzling creator. A dish that resembles one of his in another restaurant is

Alain Senderens marinates venison in a mixture of red wine, shallots, raspberry vinegar, lime juice, and parsley stems, then roasts it, and serves with juniper butter.

sure to be a copy. Robuchon copies no one; he is an original.

Because he is a consummate artist, a dinner at Robuchon's table is a feast for the eye as well as the palate. Witness the cream of cauliflower with caviar aspic or the peppered lobster with artichoke slivers sautéed in olive oil with a hint of curry; the salt cod with broad beans and soy sauce is as admirable as the simmered pig's head accompanied by the best mashed potatoes to be had; the prawn and cabbage ravioli, the sweetbreads with spinach, the spiced duck, or the roasted lamb in a salt crust are wonderfully delicious. From the crème brûlée to the bitter chocolate cake, desserts prolong the pleasure of this extraordinary state of grace. Robuchon can turn anything, even the simplest salad, into a masterpiece.

Unlike Joël Robuchon, Guy Savoy has not yet had the good fortune to find premises commensurate with his talent. He is obliged to cook in cramped kitchens and to serve his customers in a rather uncomfortable room. But the surroundings don't stop people from crowding into his establishment, for Savoy's cooking makes them forget everything else. All the dishes harmonize with extraordinary grace; the flavours, textures, and aromas are never blurred by needless sauces. On the contrary, they are highlighted by cooking juices, purées, and meat or vegetable essences that give Savoy's cuisine a rare subtlety. To whet the appetite, one might begin with a trio of variations on a theme: poached oysters, oyster mousse, and oyster aspic. Next come small morsels of lobster rolled in spinach leaves, served with mange-tout and a heavenly sauce made with the lobster carcass and coral. Then on a bed of potatoes, a nearly caramelized fillet of monkfish enhanced with a subtle shallot juice that contains neither white wine nor vinegar. Later comes a fillet of red mullet sautéed with chicken livers and bitter chicory; still later,

Guy Savoy

Alain Dutournier
Le Carré des Feuillants

sweetbreads lightly fried in butter with firm little mushrooms. Finally, chicken breast, just barely caramelized, with fresh broad beans. The grace note is a mille-feuille with cloud-light pastry cream. Those dishes are only a few of the oft-renewed array offered by Guy Savoy, who is recognized as one of the most imaginative chefs of his generation.

Another member of the same generation is Alain Dutournier, a native of southwest France. He has just left his bistro, Au Trou Gascon, to open a very attractive new restaurant called Le Carré des Feuillants, situated near the Place Vendôme in the courtyard of a historic building that once was the residence of the Countess of Castiglione, a celebrated personality of the Napoleon III era. This young Gascon is equally at ease preparing country dishes that he cleverly lightens and modernizes (roast salmon with smoked bacon, duck breast with preserved turnips, young rabbit sautéed with tiny purple artichokes, duck liver with green asparagus, cassoulet) and contemporary, innovative cuisine, which on his menu he terms "my latest ideas": crab ravioli with basil, red mullet with aubergine, caviar, chopped scallops with ginger, sweetbreads poached raw with artichokes and oysters

in a cabbage leaf, or an extraordinary gâteau of eels that is sure to change your thinking about this fish, often considered too fatty. Dutournier's wine list is one of the best and most original in Paris, particularly well stocked with exquisite, relatively inexpensive Clarets that are rarely available elsewhere.

Michel Rostang, whose father runs the well-known Bonne Auberge in Antibes, took over the premises formerly occupied by Denis, a great and extravagant chef, now deceased, whose notoriety crossed the Atlantic when he served New York *Times* food critic Craig Claiborne "the world's most expensive meal." Michel Rostang, whose cooking style admirably harmonizes the bourgeois and the modern, turned this charmless setting into one of the most elegant spots in town. You'll spend a delightful evening in this intimate, refined atmosphere, sampling such delicacies as quail's eggs stuffed with sea urchins, sautéed skate with lightly browned butter, a crusty galette of wild salmon, red mullet in a sauce made with their livers and cream, goat cheese ravioli poached in chicken broth, steamed pigeon stuffed with wild rice and foie gras, or a admirable, totally greaseless pot-au-feu.

Jacques Cagna's inn is located in a ravishing

83

Joël Robuchon's restaurant has an Old World flavour, but there is nothing old fashioned about his cuisine. Many of his fellow chefs regard Robuchon as the most original culinary talent in France.

seventeenth-century Parisian dwelling not far from Notre Dame. It is a jewel among Left Bank restaurants, with its ceiling adorned with great oaken beams and its authentic Flemish paintings and candle-lit tables. The food prepared by this very engaging young chef is modern but unaffected, light without being bland, highlighted by keen, frank flavours. His red mullet with broad beans, thyme, and coriander; his civet of pork pieces and trotters in red wine; his ravioli with mild garlic purée; the fillet of brill with lobster mousse; rib of Scottish beef sautéed with shallots; his duck in Burgundy flavoured with lemon and orange rind, and the chocolate and walnut cake are all close to perfection. If there is a last bottle of Côte-Rôtie La Mouline (a great growth from the Côtes-du-Rhône) in the cellar, don't hesitate to order it, for it is a grandiose wine!

Two young Parisian cooks have lately joined the pack of leading chefs. The first, Philippe Groult, worked for nine years with Joël Robuchon. Since his arrival at Le Manoir de Paris, food lovers have been flocking in to sample a cuisine that is reminiscent (but not imitative) of his former mentor's. His cod with anchovies, his sautéed prawns with courgettes, or the braised pork with lentils are all flawless dishes, beautifully presented, that show remarkable finesse and great personality.

The second, Régis Mahé, is a trim young man who came up to the capital after a stint in Nice as assistant to Jacques Maximin and who now presides at Le Bourdonnais. There is a sunny, southern lilt to his cooking, which is light, harmonious, and delicate, with refined and sophisticated flavour combinations (artichoke and foie gras soufflé; jellied daube of duck and pig's trotters; fillet of lamb with girolle mushrooms and herbed goat cheese ravioli; a mixed grill of red

mullet, sea bream, and sardines all cooked in their skins).

There is a venerable tradition of feminine cookery in France, but it is rare for a female chef to break out of bourgeois cuisine and make a mark with a style of her own. In Paris, Dominique Nahmias is the best of that creative breed. She and her husband, Albert, own a dinner restaurant, Olympe, with a 1930s decor that is a great favourite with show business celebrities. Dominique Nahmias is widely known thanks to her television cooking show, and her very personal, Provençal-inspired culinary style is famous. Her raw sea bream with chives, sauced with a mixture of hazelnut oil, olive oil, and soy sauce; her warm oysters with fresh pasta; the turbot with olive oil, mange-tout, peppers, and aubergine; her crayfish with artichokes; the smoked sweet-and-sour duck; and her marvellous chocolate fondant are just a few of the remarkable creations dreamed up by this young woman who had planned to study law before the kitchen won the battle for her soul.

Compared with these young chefs, Jacques Le Divellec might seem more like an elder statesman, but the exceptional youthfulness of the man who revolutionized fish cookery belies his fifty-odd years. For two decades, Le Divellec ran the best restaurant in La Rochelle on the Atlantic coast. He recently resettled in Paris near the Quai d'Orsay (the Foreign Affairs Ministry) where he opened an elegant restaurant called, not unexpectedly, Le Divellec. The place has the air of a yacht club and it is always full. Le Divellec has a positive reverence for fish, and no patience for those who destroy its delicate taste by overcooking, overstuffing, or oversaucing it.

That is not to say that he merely sautés or grills fish, then serves it up plain. His special talent is to prepare fish without spoiling its nat-

84

ural flavour, as you will see when you sample his eels, skate, red mullet, and shellfish in court bouillon; the bass roasted in its skin; oysters just barely cooked in sea-fennel; sea bream braised with fennel; or his sautéed turbot with fresh pasta and a chive-flavoured sabayon sauce.

Just a few miles from Paris, in an elegant dwelling that stands in the park surrounding Maisons-Laffitte, works another truly creative cook: François Clerc, owner of La Vieille Fontaine. This is Catherine Deneuve's favourite restaurant; she often jumps into her car to come here and indulge in Clerc's "aumonières de caviar" (caviar-filled crêpes); the salmon mille-feuille spiced with mustard seeds; skate with sea urchin cream; extraordinary pigeon pâté rolled up in a "turban" of pasta; seven-hour leg of lamb with buttered creamed cabbage; and all of Clerc's fantastic desserts.

Let's leave the capital now and chart a course for points south, on the road that passes through Burgundy and the Rhône valley, on its way to the Riviera.

Burgundy has always enjoyed an exceptional gastronomic reputation, yet, only ten or fifteen years ago, it was something of a challenge to find a really good restaurant in the region. The same old dishes were on every menu, drowning in heavy, indigestible sauces; even the most time-honored specialties were pretty wretched. The tide began to turn with the rise of nouvelle cuisine. Today, Burgundy is again a stronghold of French gastronomy, envied even by the Lyonnais, ever boastful of their superiority in the culinary sphere.

In Joigny, the old Côte Saint-Jacques has been transformed from a country inn into a ravishing luxury hotel, with sumptuous apartments overlooking the river. Owner Michel Lorain was a chef of the old school, not lacking in talent, but

Jacqueline Lorain holds the beginnings of vintage Burgundy in the family vineyard at Joigny.

inclined to fussiness. Five or six years ago, his style began to evolve, a change that was consolidated when son Jean-Michel joined his father in the kitchen after a training period with Fredy Girardet in Switzerland. Their subtle, intelligent cuisine makes La Côte Saint-Jacques one of the premier tables of France. Their carp aspic; the prawn gazpacho with cream of courgette; the scallops and foie gras steamed in parchment; the salmon cooked in a bladder; the snails with cream of parsley and tomato fondue; the pigeon with mild garlic and potato cakes; the veal kidney with artichokes and peppers; duck cooked with lentils and onions; and their wickedly tempting desserts all point up the perfection the pair has attained in calculating cooking times and harmonizing flavours. Michel Lorain's wife, Jacqueline, is an expert sommelier. She can be trusted to unearth the Meursault or Chambertin of one's dreams.

Marc Mencau's house in Saint-Père-sous-Vézelay, a comfortable middle-class villa, has an enveloping, intimate atmosphere. L'Espérance, as the restaurant is called, is set amid a small park with a stream where wild ducks paddle. His wife, Françoise, a peerless hostess, welcomes guests. Everything here is designed to delight the eye and the spirit: the attractive suites set in an antique mill, the bright and cheerful rooms, the sumptuous breakfasts, beautiful wines, and all around you the green meadows and châteaux of the Burgundy countryside.

Meneau's secret is to ignore fashion, to forget about impressing his colleagues, and to cook only to please himself and his wife. He is a careful craftsman with the soul of an artist. It is hard to decide which is more remarkable, the fertility of his imagination, the natural spontaneity of his style, the freshness of his cuisine, the clarity of the sauces, or the accuracy of the proportions and seasoning. Emotionally rooted to the land, Meneau conveys the flavours and smells of the surrounding countryside in every aspect of his cuisine: the tiny, light pâté meat balls that contain a nearly liquid filling of foie gras; the assortment of garden vegetables in fragrant chicken bouillon; the fabulous lobster with olive oil, garnished with an exquisite fennel purée; the duck liver that is nearly caramelized in mushroom cooking juices; the fillet of red mullet with watercress; his whole turbot roasted in its skin and served with onions cooked in meat juices (the match of the century!); plump and tender Loire salmon with potato straws; his stewed-rabbit tart; the truffled fillet of roasted veal with artichokes; the double chocolate (one solid, one liquid) soufflé; the cherry-vanilla ice cream; his walnut crème brûlée; or the fantastic pineapple mille-feuille. You leave the table feeling so light that you are almost tempted to start in again!

Before World War II, and up until the 1960s, Alexander Dumaine's inn, La Côte d'Or in Saulieu, was a compulsory stopping place on the road leading from Lyons to the Riviera. Celebrities from the world over visited there, but decline set in after Dumaine's retirement. The house was in a deplorable state when young

Bernard Loiseau decided to settle there a few years ago. The renovation effort is not yet complete, but with his wife, Chantal, Bernard has put in some charming suites above the newly landscaped garden. La Côte d'Or is now one of the most pleasant stopping places in Burgundy.

Bernard Loiseau is a genuinely creative chef, with a passion for innovation. He has practically banished heavy sauces from his kitchen, going so far as to use water as the liquid in some of his reductions, a technique that is not to everyone's liking. Especially memorable are a very simple but admirable vegetable fricassée fragrant with chervil; his red mullet with artichokes; "water roasted" lobster; snails with nettle butter; sea bream in red wine with shallot marmelade; braised leg of rabbit with cabbage; veal sweetbreads and kidneys with girolle mushrooms and leeks so tiny that Loiseau must have used tweezers to pull them from the garden. Outstanding wines to be sampled are Jean-Noël Gagnard's Bâtard-Montrachet, the Beaune Vignes Franches from Jacques Germain, or Simon Bize's Santenay.

Marc Meneau, a chef with the soul of an artist, cooks to please himself and his wife.

Our next halt is Lameloise, in Chagny. There is no garden or bird-song to greet the guest at the old Lameloise family hotel, set in the centre of a little town surrounded by vineyards, but the civilized pleasures of an elegant, old-fashioned decor, a warm and courteous reception, and sumptuous breakfasts more than compensate. The culinary pleasures are compliments of young Jacques Lameloise, who has taken over from his father, Jean, in the kitchen and has given a new direction to the classic house repertory. Be sure to try the terrine of young rabbit with fresh mint; his frogs sautéed with mild garlic; his herbed crayfish aspic; the Bresse pigeon cooked in a bladder, accompanied by fresh pasta with foie gras, and then finish up with strawberry mille-feuille. There to advise on wine is Georges Pertuiset, one of the most knowledgeable sommeliers in France.

Georges Blanc is as accomplished a restaurateur as he is a chef. He has transformed an utterly ordinary family inn in Vonnas, La mère Blanc—where fifty years ago his grandmother's cooking was famed throughout the region—into one of the loveliest stopovers in France. The spacious dining room with rough stone walls is decorated with a graceful Louis XIV tapestry and immense bouquets of fresh flowers. One hundred diners are all served with the same attention and courtesy. The service never allows of a false note; each meal is an exercise in faultless harmony.

Georges Blanc scours the countryside and the farms of Bresse for the local chickens, pigeons, ducks, frogs, vegetables, and herbs that give his cooking its incomparable freshness and savor. Unlike some of his peers, Blanc stubbornly refuses to abandon his kitchens; that probably explains the precision and consistency of a cuisine that is highly sophisticated despite its apparent simplicity, a skilful mix of contemporary tastes and regional traditions.

The tomato and foie gras slipped into a simple soft-boiled egg make a surprising but savoury combination. The warm frogs' legs salad with chives is judiciously seasoned with a dash of vinegar. A cold casserole of crayfish claws and tails takes on a new, disarming flavour thanks to a lemony herb sauce. Traditional potato pancakes are made sublime with the addition of smoked salmon and caviar. Don't miss the tomato stuffed with snails, sauced with an unexpected blend of herbs and white wine; the chicken liver ravioli in a highly spiced sauce made with sparkling Burgundy wine; or the casseroled Bresse chicken flanked by vegetables so fresh that they taste almost unfamiliar. Georges Blanc's lamb chops are incomparable. He marinates them for two days in garlic and olive oil, then cooks them in a lamb and veal stock thickened with butter. Magnificent. And nobody makes a better coffee meringue. All his desserts, in fact, are brilliant. The same goes for the wines, chosen by one of France's best "noses,"

The charm of the Burgundy countryside surrounds Meneau's inn, L'Esperance.

87

Marcel Périnet, who is assisted by a young English sommelier, Peter William Lowe.

Moving south, we arrive in Lyons, a rather insular city, greatly attached to its traditional gastronomy. Yet two young chefs have recently managed to introduce a somewhat different style, and their restaurants are definitely worth a visit. The first is Jean-Paul Lacombe, who succeeded his father in the kitchens of a venerable bistro loaded with charm, Léon de Lyon. Miraculously, this polished young man is just as adept at preparing the classic Lyonnais repertory (much lightened) as he is at cooking in a far more modern and personal register. He switches from one to another with remarkable flair: from the tripe with tomatoes to the terrine of foie gras and artichoke bottoms, from the traditional pike mousse to the exquisite red mullet and fennel in aspic, or from the sauté of lamb with broad beans to a delicate pink grapefruit terrine. And along with all these dishes, served in a dining room decorated with paintings and kitchen utensils that seem to belong to another age, can

be drunk the best Beaujolais on earth.

Lyons' other young innovator is thirty-year-old Philippe Chavent, established at the ovens of one of the loveliest Renaissance houses in old Lyons: La Tour Rose. It took some doing to convince the natives of Lyons that red mullet sautéed with bacon and curry, or stewed oysters (or sweetbreads) with puréed dried peas seasoned with a dash of orange pulp could be good to eat, but Chavent has managed to do so.

Saint-Etienne (located about thirty-five miles southwest of Lyons) would seem too quiet were it not the home of one of today's most fascinating young talents, Pierre Gagnaire. His restaurant is a former photographer's studio, renovated with the help of his German wife, Gabrielle. They converted it into a handsome, New York-style loft, with lacquered woodwork in strong colours, modern paintings, and a veritable forest of plants. Although he is not yet widely known, Gagnaire personifies the contemporary creative chef. He nimbly skirts all the pitfalls of "fashionable" cuisine, for he is a cook of rare subtlety. His imagination is so lively that after proposing a whole menu, he may well serve something entirely different concocted on a moment's inspiration! At any rate, nothing he makes resembles what you may find in other restaurants. Witness his prawns in beetroot juice with stewed courgettes; the gâteau of artichokes; his compote of beef with turnips and mangetout seasoned with rapeseed oil; or sliced roast lobster with broad beans in a cinnamon-and-chervil-flavoured butter. Or try his curried veal sauté with courgettes and fresh peppers, garnished with sweetbread croquettes and spinach with truffles; the salmi of wild duck braised in a bouillon of sautéed artichokes; or, finally, his fantastic hot, warm, or cold "chocolate soup." There is still not much risk of running into many foreign

Diners enjoy a late afternoon meal at Bernard Loiseau's Hôtel de la Côte d'Or on the road to the Riviera.

Christine, by the way, is an expert on the history of gastronomy. She is writing a voluminous thesis on the subject at the Sorbonne.

North, in Reims, Gerard Boyer is lord of the manor in the most sumptuous château-hotel France has seen for many a year. On fifteen acres of green lawns and gardens set in the heart of the city, the Château des Crayères was built in the nineteenth century for the owner of Pommery, the well-known Champagne label; it is luxurious, elegant, and most inviting. Gérard Boyer has prudently progressed from a classic culinary style to one that is not wholly modern, but that is personal and finely executed just the same. You could begin your meal with asparagus in puff pastry with oyster sauce, then go on to a splendid fricassée of lobster with morels or a grilled turbot garnished with a delicate, original sauce of red wine and acacia honey. Then there is the best veal kidney I've ever had the pleasure to eat, with leeks, mushrooms, and spring onions; bring the meal to a close with a selection from the loaded dessert table, and don't forget to order Champagne. The wine list offers no fewer than 118 different Champagnes! And they are less costly here than just about anywhere else.

Lille is not far away, on the road to Belgium. Robert Bardot presides at Le Flambard, the most interesting restaurant in town, as well as one of the best tables in the Nord region, located in a house that dates from the reign of Louis XIV. This ultraclassically trained cook managed to break free from his bent for complicated dishes swimming in rich sauces. His cooking has a new simplicity and robustness, yet is as technically accomplished as ever. Notable proofs of this are the warm lobster salad with tarragon, pink-roasted pigeon served with a spice-stuffed peach—an exceptionally subtle dish—and admirable ravioli stuffed with foie gras and truffles. The wine cellar, stocked with Burgundies and clarets, is sensational.

Our food lovers' pilgrimage comes to a close in Alsace, in Strasbourg, a bewitchingly beautiful city. Here love of a fine table isn't a sin, it's a virtue. The capital's top chef is Emile Jüng. He has progressed from a timid and conservative cook and has slowly but surely evolved (in Alsace, change does not happen quickly) a modern style. In a town where it was hard to find anything but sauerkraut on restaurant menus, Jüng has set a new tone for local Alsatian cuisine. In the airy and beautiful dining room of Le Crocodile, he serves a stunning goose and barley soup; a river perch in juniper-flavoured cream; a singularly tender and flavourful cockerel in a Riesling sauce; duckling with juniper and ginger (a daring but perfectly successful match); or, during hunting season, a succulent pheasant with lentils and thyme. Like Haeberlin in Illhaeusern, Emile Jüng reveres the wines of his native Alsace.

Château des Crayères, in Reims, offers one hundred varieties of Champagne on its menu.

Alain Senderens

EMINCE DE CHEVREUIL AU BEURRE DE GENIEVRE ET BAIES ROSES

ROAST VENISON WITH JUNIPER BUTTER SAUCE

MARINADE:

 1 bottle hearty red wine
 10 shallots, thinly sliced
 50 ml (2 fl oz) raspberry vinegar
 50 ml (2 fl oz) fresh lime juice
 1 large bunch parsley stems
 2 kg (2¼ lb) venison fillet, barded and tied

GARNISHES:

 3 small celeriacs (about 275 g (10 oz) each), peeled
  About 750 ml (1¼ pints) milk
  Salt and freshly ground pepper
 350 g (12 oz) pâte brisée
 1 fennel bulb, trimmed, cored, and finely diced
 2 sticks celery, finely diced
 750 g (1¼ pints) double cream
 1 red pepper, cored and finely diced
 1 green pepper, cored and finely diced
 2 large bunches parsley, all stems removed

VEGETABLE MIXTURE:

 1 large green pepper, cored and cut into 2 cm (¾ inch) squares
 1 large red pepper, cored and cut into 2 cm (¾ inch) squares
 1 large leek, washed and cut into 2 cm (¾ inch) squares
 ½ head green cabbage, cored, large leaves separated with ribs removed
  Dried rind of 1 clementine, cut into thin julienne strips
 45 ml (3 tbsp) unsalted butter
 30 ml (2 tbsp) drained pink peppercorns
  Salt and freshly ground pepper

SAUCE:

 275 g (10 oz) unsalted butter blended with 80 coarsely ground juniper berries

Prepare marinade: In a large flameproof casserole, combine wine, shallots, vinegar, lime juice, and parsley. Add venison and marinate at cool room temperature, turning occasionally, for 4 hours.

Prepare garnishes: Halve celeriacs crossways and cut a small slice from the bottom of each so they sit flat. Rinse well. With a melon baller, carefully scoop out inside of each half, leaving a 1 cm (½ inch) shell. Place celeriacs in a medium saucepan and add enough milk to cover. Season with salt and pepper and bring to the boil. Simmer over medium heat for about 30 minutes or until celeriac 'cups' are tender. Drain, rinse, and set aside.

Heat oven to 200C (400F) gas 6.

Roll out pastry to 3 mm (⅛ inch) thick. With a 13 cm (5 inch) round or fluted pastry cutter, stamp out 12 rounds (you may have to re-roll the dough). Line 12 7.5 cm (3 inch) round or fluted tart tins with pastry circles. Line each mould with aluminium foil, fill with baking beans, and place in the freezer for about 10 minutes. Arrange tart tins on a baking sheet and bake for 10 minutes. Remove foil and beans and continue baking for about 10 minutes or until pastry is fully cooked and golden brown. Unmould tart shells on to a rack to cool.

In a saucepan of boiling salted water, blanch the fennel and celery together for 2 minutes. Drain well and place in a small saucepan with 100 ml (4 fl oz) double cream.

In another saucepan of boiling salted water, blanch red and green peppers for 2 minutes. Drain well and place in a small saucepan with 100 ml (4 fl oz) double cream.

Cook parsley leaves in a steamer for 6 minutes. Remove from steamer and, when cool enough to handle, squeeze out as much liquid as possible. Place in a small saucepan with 175 ml (6 fl oz) double cream.

Set all 3 saucepans over medium heat and cook each mixture for about 20 minutes or until cream reduces and thickens and vegetables are tender. Season with salt and pepper to taste.

Place celeriacs, hollowed side up, in an ovenproof dish just large enough to hold them and fill with fennel-celery mixture. Pour remaining double cream into the dish and braise in the oven for 15 minutes.

Prepare vegetable mixture: In a large saucepan of boiling salted water, blanch green and red pepper, leek, cabbage, and clementine rind for 4 minutes. Drain well. In a large frying pan melt butter. Add blanched vegetables and cook over medium heat, stirring occasionally, for about 15 minutes or until tender. Stir in pink peppercorns and season to taste with salt and pepper.

Prepare venison and sauce: Remove venison from casserole and dry well with kitchen towels. Set casserole over medium-high heat and boil marinade for about 40 minutes or until reduced to 100 ml (4 fl oz). Strain through a fine-mesh sieve set over a medium saucepan.

Season venison with salt and pepper and roast it in the oven for 30 minutes (it will be quite rare). Transfer to a cutting board, cover with aluminium foil, and let rest in a warm place for 15 minutes.

Bring strained marinade to the boil over high heat and cook for about 5 minutes or until reduced to 50 ml (2 fl oz). Reduce heat to medium low and whisk in juniper butter, a few spoonfuls at a time; strain and season with salt and pepper.

To serve: Re-heat tart shells and celeriac in the oven. Re-heat vegetable mixture, peppers in cream, and creamed parsley. Fill 6 tart shells with peppers, and 6 with parsley mixture. Drain stuffed celeriac. Slice venison and place on 6 large heated plates. Garnish each serving with a stuffed celeriac, one of each tart, and a large spoonful of the vegetable mixture. Carefully re-heat the sauce, if necessary, and spoon on to plates or pass separately in a sauceboat.

Makes 6 servings

Joël Robuchon

MIGNONNETTES DE CHEVREUIL POELEES A L'AIGRE-DOUX

SWEET AND SOUR VENISON MIGNONNETTES

40	g (1½ oz) fresh truffle, finely chopped
90	ml (6 tbsp) chopped parsley
750	g (1½ lb) venison fillet, trimmed and cut into 12 slices, plus 25 g (1 oz) venison, minced
2	egg yolks size 2, lightly beaten
100	g (4 oz) unsalted butter
15	ml (1 tbsp) finely chopped shallots
15	g (½ oz) black chanterelles, rinsed, dried, and finely chopped, or substitute other thin, membraned wild mushroom
15	g (½ oz) flat leaf parsley, stems removed
25	g (1 oz) foie gras
25	g (1 oz) minced lean pork
50	g (2 oz) fresh ravioli dough
3	slices fresh pineapple, cut 2 cm (¾ inch) thick
	Salt and freshly ground pepper
15	ml (1 tbsp) safflower oil
30	ml (2 tbsp) aged wine vinegar
3	juniper berries
100	ml (4 fl oz) game or chicken stock
225	g (8 oz) cooked cranberries

In a small bowl, combine 25g (1 oz) finely chopped truffle and chopped parsley. Dip each slice of venison in egg yolks, then coat with parsley-truffle mixture. Reserve.

In a small, heavy saucepan, melt 15 ml (1 tbsp) butter. Add shallots and cook until soft, but not browned. Remove and reserve in a small bowl. Repeat procedure with wild mushrooms; remove from heat and combine with shallots. Blanch parsley in 225 ml (8 fl oz) boiling, salted water for 1 minute; drain and chop finely. Add to mushroom-shallot mixture along with foie gras, remaining chopped truffle, minced venison, and pork. Combine well.

On a floured work surface, roll out ravioli dough as thin as possible and shape into 2 equal rectangles. With a small spoon, spoon mushroom mixture at 12 even intervals on one of the rectangles. With a brush dipped in water, moisten dough around each spoonful of filling and cover with second dough rectangle. Press pastry together between each ravioli and cut with a small pastry cutter.

Cut pineapple slices into quarters to give 12 small sections. In a heavy frying pan, melt 30 ml (2 tbsp) butter. Add pineapple and sauté for about 1 minute; remove from heat and cover.

Bring 1.5 litres (2½ pints) water to the boil with 1.25 ml (¼ tsp) salt. Add ravioli and poach for 5 to 8 minutes; drain. In a small, heavy saucepan, heat 30 ml (2 tbsp) butter, add ravioli and keep warm.

Season venison with salt and pepper to taste. In a large, heavy frying pan, melt oil and 30 ml (2 tbsp) butter. Add venison and sauté for about 3 minutes on each side; the meat should be pink. Transfer to a heated dish and keep warm. Degrease the pan and deglaze with 15-30 ml (1-2 tbsp) wine vinegar. Add juniper berries and stock. Season to taste. Re-heat cranberries.

To serve: Strain sauce and spoon a little on to each of 4 heated plates. Arrange 3 alternate slices of venison and pineapple on each plate. Place a spoonful of cranberries on each pineapple slice and arrange ravioli in centre of plate. Serve immediately.

Makes 4 servings

Joël Robuchon alternates venison and pineapple to achieve a sweet-and-sour taste.

Joël Robuchon

SALADE DE HOMARD EN BOLERO

LOBSTER SALAD WITH TOMATO, APPLE, AND AVOCADO

2.5	litres (4½ pints) water
1	large carrot, sliced
1	large onion, sliced
1	stick celery, sliced
1	large bouquet garni
100	ml (4 fl oz) wine vinegar or 300 ml (½ pint) white wine
15	whole peppercorns
5	ml (1 tsp) salt
4	450 g (1 lb) lobsters
75	ml (3 fl oz) wine vinegar
100	ml (4 fl oz) groundnut oil
25	ml (1½ tbsp) crème fraîche
	Salt and freshly ground pepper
2	large, ripe tomatoes, skinned
1	Golden Delicious apple, peeled
1	large, ripe avocado, peeled
45	ml (3 tbsp) fresh lemon juice
15	ml (1 tbsp) sunflower oil
20	ml (4 tsp) snipped fresh chives
20	ml (4 tsp) fresh chervil leaves

In a large, non-aluminium stockpot, combine water, carrot, onion, celery, bouquet garni, 100 ml (4 fl oz) vinegar, peppercorns, and salt. Bring to the boil over high heat, then reduce heat to medium and simmer for 30 minutes. Strain court bouillon into another large stockpot.

Return liquid to the boil over high heat. Add lobsters, head first. Reduce heat to medium and cook lobsters for 6 minutes. Remove from heat and let lobsters cool in the cooking liquid.

While lobsters cool, prepare salad. Pour 75 ml (3 fl oz) vinegar into a small bowl and whisk in groundnut oil, a little at a time. When all oil has been incorporated, whisk in crème fraîche. Season to taste with salt and pepper.

Halve tomatoes and carefully seed them without tearing the flesh. Using a tiny melon baller, carve out small rounds of tomato flesh. (If you don't have a melon baller, cut tomatoes into 0.5 cm (¼ inch) dice.) Place in a medium bowl.

Cut the apple and avocado in the same fashion (either in tiny balls or 0.5 cm (¼ inch) dice). In a small bowl, toss the apple and avocado with lemon juice to coat thoroughly; drain well and add to tomatoes. Cover and refrigerate.

When lobsters are cool enough to handle, remove them from their cooking liquid and dry well with kitchen towels. Separate the tails, forelegs, and claws from the bodies. Crack claws and try to remove meat in one piece. Remove tail and leg meat from shells. Place all lobster meat on a plate, cover and refrigerate until well chilled. Reserve carcasses and reserve shells for another use.

Pour about 45 ml (3 tbsp) of vinaigrette on to each plate. Toss chilled lobster meat with remaining vinaigrette; drain lightly. Slice lobster tails into medallions 0.5 cm (¼ inch) thick; remove any dark parts of intestine. Arrange medallions in a circle in the centre of each plate. Place claws at the top of the plate and leg meat in the centre of the medallions.

Toss tomato, apple, and avocado salad with sunflower oil and sprinkle a large soupspoonful over each serving. Garnish each plate with 5 ml (1 tsp) chives and 5 ml (1 tsp) chervil.

Makes 4 servings

Robuchon's cold lobster salad includes tomato, apple, and avocado.

Guy Savoy

OURSINS AUX CROSNES

SEA URCHINS WITH ARTICHOKES

4   large artichokes, stalks and dark outer leaves
    removed
    Freshly squeezed lemon juice plus 1 lemon,
    halved
45 ml (3 tbsp) plain flour
8   large or 12 small sea urchins
60 -75 ml (4-5 tbsp) cold unsalted butter
    Freshly ground pepper

Remove all leaves from artichokes, cutting them about 4 cm (1½ inches) from base, level with choke; rub cut surfaces with lemon juice to prevent discoloration. Beginning at stalk ends, use a sharp knife to cut around base and sides, trimming away all traces of dark green leaves. With knife held at an angle, trim tops around chokes; rub cut surfaces with lemon juice as you go.

Place trimmed artichoke bottoms in a medium, stainless steel saucepan and cover with cold water. Whisk in flour. Squeeze juice from lemon halves and add juice and lemon to pan. Bring to the boil over high heat. Reduce heat to medium and simmer for about 20 minutes or until artichokes are just tender when pierced with a knife. Let artichokes cool in cooking liquid.

Meanwhile, prepare sea urchins. Hold one urchin in a towel, with its mouth facing you. Insert the tip of pointy kitchen scissors into mouth. Cut out a large circle around mouth, grasp underside with scissors, and lift it out. Invert urchin over a fine-mesh sieve, set over a small saucepan, and gently shake out juices. With a small spoon, scoop out orange roe, which clings to inside of urchin shell in a star pattern, and place in a bowl. Repeat with remaining urchins.

Gently rinse roe in cold water and drain on kitchen towels. Add roe to strained urchin juices in saucepan.

Remove artichokes from cooking liquid and drain on kitchen towels. With a small spoon, scoop out hairy chokes. Thinly slice artichoke bottoms and divide among 4 serving plates, fanning the slices decoratively.

Warm urchin roe over low heat. Carefully remove roe with a slotted spoon and divide among plates.

Bring urchin liquid to the boil over high heat. Remove from heat and whisk in butter, 30 ml (2 tbsp) at a time. Season sauce with pepper and lemon juice to taste and spoon it over artichokes and urchin roe. Serve immediately.

Makes 4 servings

Ed. note: The original version of this recipe calls for crosnes, a small root vegetable not widely available. The chef suggests using artichoke bottoms in their place. Sea urchin roe is available from fishmongers catering for Japanese restaurants.

Guy Savoy combines sea urchins and a vegetable in this unusual dish.

Guy Savoy

SOUPE A L'EMINCE DE POISSON
SLICED FISH SOUP WITH SAFFRON

450	g (1 lb) fish bones, preferably a mixture of sole and eel, well-rinsed
1	onion, sliced
8	parsley stems
1.75	litres (3 pints) cold water
45	ml (3 tbsp) olive oil
1	carrot, finely diced
1	onion, finely chopped
1	leek, white and tender green, well-washed and finely chopped
1	ripe tomato, skinned, seeded, and chopped
1	bouquet garni
1	clove garlic, finely chopped
	Pinch of saffron threads
45	ml (3 tbsp) double cream
	Pinch of thyme
	Salt and freshly ground pepper
350	g (12 oz) fish fillets: 1 small piece monkfish, thinly sliced; 1 small piece red snapper, unskinned and cut into pieces; 1 small piece sole or whiting, cut into 0.5 cm (¼ inch) strips
	Fresh chervil leaves

In a large stockpot, combine fish bones, onion, parsley stems, and water; bring to the boil over medium-high heat. Reduce heat to medium and simmer stock, skimming frequently, for 15 minutes. Strain stock through a very fine mesh sieve.

In a large casserole, heat olive oil. Add the carrot, onion, and leek and cook over medium heat, stirring occasionally, for about 10 minutes or until vegetables are soft. Add tomato and cook 1 minute longer. Stir in fish stock, bouquet garni, and garlic; bring to the boil over high heat. With a ladle, skim surface of soup until it is clear of foam. Add saffron and simmer soup over medium heat for 40 minutes.

Meanwhile, heat oven to 190C (375F) gas 5.

Place 4 large ovenproof soup plates or bowls on a baking sheet and heat in the oven until very hot.

Stir cream and thyme into soup and season with salt and pepper to taste. Ladle 225 ml (8 fl oz) soup into each bowl and evenly distribute sliced fish among bowls. Bake in heated oven for exactly 2 minutes. Fill bowls with remaining soup, sprinkle with chervil leaves, and serve immediately.

Makes 4 servings

Facing page: Guy Savoy's fish-and-saffron soup.

Right: Alain Dutournier bakes hen pheasants in a flower-shaped tart.

Alain Dutournier

CROUSTADE DE POULE FAISAN AUX CHAMPIGNONS SAUVAGES
HEN PHEASANTS WITH WILD MUSHROOMS

2	hen pheasants, boned, with bones chopped and reserved
5	ml (1 tsp) Dijon-style mustard
1.25	ml (¼ tsp) juniper berries, ground
1.25	ml (¼ tsp) grated nutmeg
1	clove, ground
50	ml (2 fl oz) port wine
300	ml (½ pint) white wine
	Salt and freshly ground pepper
100	g (4 oz) unsalted butter, plus 50 g (2 oz) unsalted butter, melted
2	carrots, peeled and chopped
5	shallots, chopped, plus 15 ml (1 tbsp) chopped shallot
40	g (1½ oz) dried cèpes, soaked in water and drained, plus 350 g (12 oz) fresh cèpes
225	ml (8 fl oz) crème fraîche
45	ml (3 tbsp) chopped parsley
350	g (12 oz) fresh girolles
350	g (12 oz) fresh pieds de mouton
5	to 8, 20.5 x 40 cm (8 x 16 inch) sheets phyllo or thin strudel dough

(Recipe continued overleaf)

Georges Blanc

ROSACE DE TOMATE FARCIE AUX CHAMPIGNONS, AUX NAVETS FONDANTS ET AUX ESCARGOTS BEURRE VERT PRE

SNAIL-AND-MUSHROOM-STUFFED TOMATO AND TURNIP ROSACE WITH GREEN HERB BUTTER

SNAIL-AND-MUSHROOM-STUFFED TOMATO:

5	firm, ripe, medium tomatoes, skinned
100	g (4 oz) mushrooms, trimmed and finely chopped
	juice of ½ lemon
30	ml (2 tbsp) unsalted butter
15	ml (1 tbsp) finely chopped shallots
1	small clove garlic, finely chopped
12	snails, without shells, or substitute 175 g (6 oz) fish, shellfish, or meat
2.5	ml (½ tsp) Dijon-style mustard
	Salt and freshly ground pepper
5	fl oz (¼ pint) crème fraîche
15	ml (1 tbsp) finely snipped fresh chives
15	ml (1 tbsp) olive oil

GREEN HERB BUTTER:

1	small bunch parsley, stemmed and coarsely chopped
½	bunch watercress, thick stems removed and coarsely chopped
20	chives, coarsely snipped
15	shoots of chervil, coarsely chopped, plus 4 shoots, stems removed, optional
100	ml (4 fl oz) cold water
105	ml (7 tbsp) cold unsalted butter, cut into small pieces
2.5	ml (½ tsp) red wine vinegar
	Salt and freshly ground pepper

FONDANT TURNIPS:

225	g (8 oz) small white turnips, peeled and cut into 16 even-sized pieces
15	ml (1 tbsp) unsalted butter

Prepare snail-and-mushroom-stuffed tomato: Cut 4 tomatoes into even quarters. Remove and discard interior, seeds, and juice. Lightly salt tomatoes and set aside. Remove seeds and juice from remaining tomato, then chop finely and reserve.

In a small saucepan, place mushrooms, lemon juice, and 15 ml (1 tbsp) butter. Add enough water to partially cover mushrooms and cook, covered, over medium heat for about 8 minutes. Remove from heat and drain.

In a heavy saucepan, melt 15 ml (1 tbsp) butter. Add shallots and garlic and cook until lightly coloured. Add snails and 15 ml (1 tbsp) reserved chopped tomato. Cook over low heat for about 3 minutes. Add mushrooms and stir well. Season with mustard and salt and pepper to taste. Cook over low heat, add crème fraîche, and simmer for 5 minutes. Remove from heat and add chives.

Prepare green herb butter: In a small saucepan, place parsley, watercress, chives, chopped chervil, and cold water. Bring to a slow boil and cook about 3 minutes. Remove from heat and set aside to cool. Drain, reserving liquid, and transfer herbs to a food processor or blender. Process until puréed and add about 20 ml (4 tsp) of reserved cooking liquid to smooth mixture. Transfer puréed herbs to a small, heavy saucepan and cook, whisking constantly, over low heat. Add butter, a few pieces at a time. Season with vinegar and salt and pepper to taste. Transfer sauce to blender and process for 1 to 2 seconds. Keep sauce warm or re-heat at serving time.

Prepare fondant turnips: With a small kitchen knife, trim turnips to olive shapes. Cook in boiling salted water for about 3 minutes; strain and transfer to a bowl of ice water to cool.

Drain and set aside.

To serve: Heat oven to 170C (300F) gas 2. Drain excess liquid from quartered tomatoes and place them in an ovenproof dish with 25 ml (1½ tbsp) reserved chopped tomatoes. Heat in heated oven for about 3 minutes. Reheat snails.

In a heavy saucepan, melt 15 ml (1 tbsp) butter. Add turnips and cook over medium heat for 4 to 5 minutes or until warmed, but not coloured. Salt to taste. Reheat green herb butter and spoon it onto 4 warmed shallow plates. With 2 oval soupspoons, form warm snail mixture into 16 even ovals; place 4 ovals in a spoke pattern on each plate. Cover with warm tomato quarters, pointed ends facing rim of plate, and intersperse decoratively with fondant turnips. Dip a brush into olive oil and lightly paint each tomato petal. Place 5 ml (1 tsp) of reserved chopped tomato in centre of each plate. Sprinkle with chervil, if desired. Serve immediately.

Makes 4 servings

In George Blanc's brilliantly coloured dish, tomato quarters are stuffed with snails and mushrooms and arranged in herb butter.

Michel and Jean-Michel Lorain

LA SUITE DES TROIS DESSERTS AU CHOCOLAT ET A LA MENTHE FRAICHE

TRIO OF CHOCOLATE DESSERTS WITH FRESH MINT

ICE CREAM:

475	ml (16 fl oz) milk
52	ml (3½ tbsp) honey
50	g (2 oz) plain chocolate, chopped
6	egg yolks
75	ml (5 tbsp) granulated sugar
75	g (3 oz) unsweetened cocoa powder

CREME ANGLAISE:

475	ml (16 fl oz) milk
1	vanilla pod, split
6	egg yolks
75	ml (5 tbsp) granulated sugar
1.25	ml (¼ tsp) chopped fresh mint leaves

MOUSSE CAKE:

375	g (13 oz) plain chocolate, chopped
45	ml (3 tbsp) double cream plus 225 ml (8 fl oz) double cream, whipped until stiff
2	eggs, separated
15	ml (1 tbsp) plus 5 ml (1 tsp) granulated sugar

SOUFFLE:

	Butter and sugar, for the moulds
2	eggs, separated, plus 2 egg whites
75	ml (5 tbsp) plus 25 ml (1½ tbsp) granulated sugar
30	ml (2 tbsp) unsweetened cocoa powder
	Fresh mint leaves

114

A trio of chocolate desserts from Michel and Jean-Michel Lorain.

Prepare ice cream: In a medium saucepan, bring milk and honey to the boil over medium-high heat. Remove from heat, add chopped chocolate, and stir until melted. In a bowl, whisk egg yolks with sugar until thoroughly blended; whisk in cocoa. Gradually whisk in hot milk mixture. Return to saucepan and cook over medium-low heat, whisking constantly for about 10 minutes or until thickened. Transfer to a large bowl and refrigerate until cold. Pour cooled mixture into an ice cream machine and freeze according to the manufacturer's directions.

Prepare crème anglaise: In a medium saucepan, scald milk with vanilla pod. In a bowl, whisk egg yolks with sugar. Gradually whisk hot milk into yolk mixture. Return mixture to saucepan and cook over medium-low heat, stirring constantly with a wooden spoon, for about 15 minutes or until custard thickens. Pour custard into a bowl, stir in mint, and refrigerate until cold.

Prepare mousse cake: In a double boiler, melt 200 g (7 oz) chocolate. Meanwhile, use a pencil to trace three 20 cm (8 inch) circles on a large sheet of grease-proof paper. When chocolate is melted and completely smooth, pour one-third of it into centre of each circle. With a palette knife spread chocolate into a thin, even layer, following traced patterns. Let cool at room temperature until set.

In a double boiler, heat remaining chocolate and 45 ml (3 tbsp) cream, stirring occasionally, until chocolate is melted. Whisk in egg yolks and transfer mixture to a large bowl; cool to room temperature.

Meanwhile, in a large bowl, whisk egg whites with sugar until stiff peaks form. When chocolate mixture is cool, fold in whisked whites. When whites are almost fully incorporated, fold in whipped double cream.

Carefully remove chocolate discs from greaseproof paper. Reserve most perfect disc for top of cake. Place a disc on a large plate and spoon half the mousse mixture on to it. With a palette knife spread mousse to edges. Cover with a second disc and spread with remaining mousse. Top with last disc and refrigerate until serving time.

Prepare soufflé: Heat oven to 230C (450F) gas 8. Butter six 150g (5 oz) ramekins and dust lightly with sugar; refrigerate.

In a small bowl, whisk egg yolks with 40 g (2½ tbsp) sugar until pale and fluffy; whisk in 15 ml (1 tbsp) cocoa. In a large bowl, whisk egg whites with remaining sugar until stiff peaks form. Fold in remaining cocoa. Stir a little of the whites into the egg yolk mixture to lighten, then fold yolk mixture into whites until well combined. Arrange prepared ramekins on a baking sheet, fill with soufflé mixture, and bake on the bottom rack of the oven for about 12 minutes or until puffed and set.

To serve: Strain crème anglaise and pour it on to 6 large dessert plates. Heat a large slicing knife under hot water, wipe dry, and cut mousse cake into 6 slices. Place a slice of cake and a large scoop of ice cream on each plate. As soon as soufflés are ready, unmould them, turn right-side-up, and arrange on plates. Garnish each serving with fresh mint leaves and serve immediately.

Makes 6 servings

Ed. note: In this dessert, three chocolate confections of different temperature and texture are served together.

Bernard Loiseau

LE RAGOUT DE LEGUMES AU CERFEUIL
VEGETABLE STEW WITH CHERVIL

8	to 10 baby carrots
3	to 4 small white turnips, peeled
2	to 3 young courgettes
10	to 12 small pickling onions and/or spring onions, trimmed
75	g (3 oz) unsalted butter
350	g (12 oz) green cabbage, thinly sliced, or broccoli florets
½	medium red pepper, cut into 0.5 cm (¼ inch) dice
2.5	ml (½ tsp) olive oil
100	ml (4 fl oz) cold water
5	ml (1 tsp) fresh lemon juice
	Salt and freshly ground pepper
5	ml (1 tsp) fresh chervil leaves

With a small kitchen knife, slice the carrots, turnips, and courgettes into similar-size ovals. In each of 4 small saucepans, place carrots, onions, turnips, and courgettes and add enough water barely to cover vegetables. Add 15 ml (1 tbsp) butter to each pan and cook over medium heat for 3 to 7 minutes. Blanch cabbage in boiling water for 1 minute. In a small frying pan, sauté red pepper in olive oil over medium heat for about 1 minute.

In a large, heavy-based saucepan, melt remaining 30 ml (2 tbsp) butter. Add carrots, turnips, courgettes and onions and sauté over medium heat for about 1 minute or until pale golden in colour, but not browned. Deglaze with cold water and lemon juice. Add blanched cabbage, red pepper, and salt and pepper to taste. Serve in a deep casserole garnished with chervil.

Makes 4 servings

115

Overleaf: The simplest of ingredients from the garden are transformed by Bernard Loiseau into a sophisticated vegetable stew.

ROMANÉ
VOSNE
J. Drouhin
Beaune
FRANÇAISE NON RECONSTITUÉE
française non Reconstituée · Appellation
& J. Chambon
Seuls propriétaires

LE FEUILLETE A L'ORANGE

GRAND MARNIER ICE CREAM IN PUFF PASTRY WITH ORANGES AND

ICE CREAM:
- 750 ml (1¼ pints) milk
- 150 g (5 oz) granulated sugar
- 1 vanilla pod, split lengthways
- 12 egg yolks
- 5 ml (1 tsp) Grand Marnier

CARAMELIZED ORANGE RIND:
- 6 small naval oranges, well-washed
- 300 g (10 oz) sugar
- 300 ml (½ pint) water
- 30 ml (2 tbsp) grenadine

PASTRY AND SAUCE:
- 450 g (1 lb) frozen puff pastry, defrosted
- 1.25 kg (2½ lb) raspberries
- Icing sugar
- 2 small naval oranges
- 30 ml (2 tbsp) unsalted butter
- 30 ml (2 tbsp) granulated sugar
- Fresh mint leaves

Prepare ice cream mixture: In a medium saucepan, combine milk with 75 g (2½ oz) sugar and the vanilla pod; bring to the boil over medium heat.

Meanwhile, in a medium bowl, whisk egg yolks with remaining 75 g (2½ oz) sugar until pale and thick. Whisk hot milk into egg yolk mixture until thoroughly blended, then return mixture to saucepan. Cook over medium heat, stirring constantly with a wooden spoon, for about 12 minutes or until mixture is thick enough to coat the back of the spoon. Remove from heat and strain into a bowl. Let cool slightly, then refrigerate until well chilled.

Prepare caramelized orange rind: With a vegetable peeler or a sharp knife, strip rinds from oranges and cut into fine julienne. Reserve oranges. In a medium, heavy-based saucepan, bring the sugar and water to the boil over medium-high heat. When the sugar has dissolved, add julienned rinds and grenadine and cook over medium heat for about 15 minutes or until rinds are lightly caramelized. With a wire skimmer or a fork, transfer rinds to a lightly oiled wire rack to cool.

Heat oven to 200C (400F) gas 6.

With a sharp knife, finely chop caramelized rinds. Add them to ice cream mixture and stir in Grand Marnier. Pour mixture into an ice cream machine and freeze according to the manufacturer's directions.

Prepare pastry and sauce: With a 11.25 cm (4½ inch) fluted pastry cutter, stamp out 8 rounds from the puff pastry. Set rounds on a heavy baking sheet and bake in heated oven for about 12 minutes or until puffed and browned. Transfer to a rack to cool.

Purée raspberries in a food mill or a food processor. Strain purée into a bowl and sift in icing sugar to taste. Refrigerate sauce.

With a sharp knife, peel the 2 oranges and the 6 that were stripped of rind; remove all bitter white pith. Slice in between membranes to remove sections. In a large frying pan, melt butter over medium-low heat. Add orange sections and sugar and cook, tossing constantly, until warmed through, about 1 minute. Remove from heat.

Assemble dessert: Cut pastries in half horizontally. Sift icing sugar over pastry tops. Spoon raspberry sauce on to 8 plates, place a pastry bottom on each; and surround with orange sections. Place a scoop of ice cream on each pastry and cover with sugared tops. Garnish each serving with mint leaves and serve immediately.

Makes 8 servings

Bernard Loiseau's Grand Marnier ice cream with raspberry sauce.

Jacques Chibois

LE PAPILLON DE LANGOUSTINES A LA CHIFFONADE DE MESCLUN

BUTTERFLY OF LANGOUSTINES WITH BASIL CHIFFONADE

BUTTERFLY OF LANGOUSTINES:

12	to 20 fresh langoustines or large prawns, unpeeled
	Salt and freshly ground pepper
1.25	litres (2¼ pints) water
225	g (8 oz) French beans, trimmed
1	bunch lamb's lettuce, watercress, or other salad greens
1	to 2 small courgettes, sliced into thin matchstick strips
8	whole fresh basil leaves, plus 8 fresh basil leaves, cut widthways into thin strips for chiffonade
8	small cherry tomatoes

CITRUS VINAIGRETTE:

2	medium oranges, peeled, membrane removed, and divided into segments
1	lemon, peeled, membrane removed, and divided into segments
100	ml (4 fl oz) olive oil
10	fresh basil leaves, optional
1.25	ml (¼ tsp) ground coriander seeds
1	ripe tomato, skinned, seeded, and finely chopped
	Salt and freshly ground pepper

Prepare butterfly of langoustines: Steam langoustines for 8 to 10 minutes. From 4 langoustines, remove only tail shell; remove entire shell from remaining langoustines. Place all langoustines in an ovenproof dish and season with salt and pepper.

In a large enamel or stainless-steel saucepan, bring water to the boil. Add 5 ml (1 tsp) salt and French beans; blanch for 5 to 8 minutes or until just tender. With a slotted spoon, transfer beans to a bowl of iced water to cool; drain immediately.

Prepare citrus vinaigrette: In a blender, combine orange and lemon segments, olive oil, basil, and coriander. Blend to emulsify. In a small saucepan, combine orange mixture, chopped tomato, and salt and pepper to taste. Set aside.

To serve: Heat oven to 170C (325F) gas 3. Divide salad greens and arrange in centre of 4 plates. Place French beans on both sides of plate so they extend from centre in a fan-like pattern; arrange courgettes in a similar fan-like pattern at bottom of plate.

Re-heat langoustines in heated oven for about 3 minutes. Heat citrus vinaigrette over low heat, whisking, until warm. Arrange peeled langoustines at top end of plates and place one whole langoustine in centre of each plate, with claws forming a triangle at top. Place 1 basil leaf on each side of langoustine and a cherry tomato near both clusters of beans. Coat langoustines with warm citrus vinaigrette and sprinkle with basil chiffonade. Serve immediately.

Makes 4 servings

Overleaf: Nouvelle cuisine often recalls the style of Japanese food arrangement. In this dish by Jacques Chibois the steamed langoustines are coated with hot citrus vinaigrette and sprinkled with basil chiffonade.

Pierre Gagnaire

TAMPURA DE LANGOUSTINES, POMMES DE TERRE SAUTEES AU BEURRE CLARIFIE, BEURRE FONDU A LA CANNELLE ET CIBOULETTE

LANGOUSTINE TEMPURA WITH CHIVE AND CINNAMON BUTTER

LANGOUSTINE TEMPURA.

8	large langoustines or prawns, peeled
100	ml (4 fl oz) double cream
1	large or 2 small green cabbage leaves
2	small baking potatoes, peeled, sliced 3mm (⅛ inch) thick, and soaked in cold water overnight
100	g (4 oz) unsalted butter, clarified, plus 15 ml (1 tbsp) butter, at room temperature
475	g (16 fl oz) vegetable oil
50	g (2 oz) plain flour
2	radishes, thinly sliced, in 15 ml (1 tbsp) safflower oil

CHIVE AND CINNAMON BUTTER:

30	ml (2 tbsp) cold water
	Pinch of salt
1.25	ml (¼ tsp) ground cinnamon
60	ml (4 tbsp) cold unsalted butter, cut into pieces
15	ml (1 tbsp) fresh snipped chives

122

Prepare langoustine tempura: Heat oven to 190C (375F) gas 5. Place langoustines and double cream in a medium bowl; set aside. Blanch cabbage in 475 ml (16 fl oz) boiling, salted water for 2 to 3 minutes. Transfer to a bowl of iced water to cool; drain and set aside.

Drain and dry potato slices and coat with clarified butter. Arrange potatoes, in a single layer, on a large, heavy baking sheet and bake in heated oven for 15 to 20 minutes or until crisp and golden. Remove from oven and keep warm.

Prepare chive and cinnamon butter: In a small, heavy saucepan, heat water, salt, and cinnamon over low heat. Whisk in butter, a few pieces at a time. When butter is incorporated, add chives. Remove from heat and keep warm.

To serve: In a heavy frying pan or saucepan, heat oil to 190C (375F). One at a time, remove langoustines from cream and coat lightly with flour; deep-fry in hot oil for 1 to 2 minutes. With a slotted spoon, remove langoustines and cut into small pieces; salt to taste. In a heavy saucepan, heat 15 ml (1 tbsp) butter over low heat. Add cabbage leaves and cook for 3 to 5 minutes without browning.

Place cabbage in centre of 2 heated plates. Arrange potato slices on top and surround with pieces of langoustine. Decorate plates with radish slivers and a ribbon of chive and cinnamon butter.

Makes 2 servings

Pierre Gagnaire

CONSOMME GLACE GERMINY, FILET DE PIGEON AU JUS DE BETTERAVE

PIGEON BREASTS WITH GERMINY MOUSSE AND BEETROOT CREAM SAUCE

GERMINY MOUSSE:

175	ml (6 fl oz) gelatinous beef or veal stock
3	egg yolks
15	ml (1 tbsp) port
100	ml (4 fl oz) double cream, stiffly whipped

PIGEON BREASTS AND VEGETABLES:

1	carrot, cut into 0.5 cm (¼ inch) matchsticks
225	ml (8 fl oz) boiling stock or salted water
2	large spinach leaves, stemmed and finely shredded
1.25	ml (¼ tsp) soy sauce
	Salt and freshly ground pepper
2	225 g (8 oz) pigeon breasts
5	ml (1 tsp) unsalted butter
1	shallot, finely chopped
	Pinch of coarse salt

Preceding overleaf: Pierre Gagnaire's langoustine tempura.

PETIT SALE DE CANARD AUX LENTILLES

SALT-CURED DUCK LEGS WITH VEGETABLES AND LENTILS

6 large duck legs, about 225 g (8 oz) each (from foie gras ducks)

50 g (2 oz) coarse salt

1 medium carrot, thinly sliced, plus 3 medium carrots, cut into large ovals or thickly sliced, plus 1 carrot, finely diced

1 onion, studded with 3 cloves

1 bouquet garni, made with celery, leek, bay leaves, parsley stems, and thyme

1 star anise pod

900 ml (1½ pints) plus 475 ml (16 fl oz) water

3 medium turnips, cut into large ovals or sixths

3 red-skinned potatoes, cut into large ovals or sixths

15 ml (1 tbsp) goose fat

2 shallots, finely chopped

25 g (1 oz) pancetta, cut into julienne strips

2 Italian plum tomatoes, skinned, seeded, and coarsely chopped

2 garlic cloves, finely chopped

100 g (4 oz) green lentils

1 bouquet garni

Salt and freshly ground pepper

6 large cabbage leaves, central ribs removed

Michel Trama serves duck legs with vegetable-and-lentil stuffed cabbage leaf.

Place duck legs in a large ovenproof dish and rub with salt. Cover and refrigerate, turning occasionally, for 12 hours or overnight.

In a large saucepan, combine thinly sliced carrot, onion, bouquet garni, star anise, and 900 ml (1½ pints) water. Bring to the boil, cover partially, and simmer over medium heat for 1 hour. Strain liquid into a large ovenproof casserole.

Heat oven to 180C (350F) gas 4.

Rinse salt from duck legs with cold water and pat dry with paper towels. Add duck to casserole and bring to the boil over medium heat. Cover casserole and bake in heated oven for 1 hour. Add carrot ovals, turnips, and potatoes and bake for about 20 minutes or until duck and vegetables are tender.

In a large saucepan, melt goose fat. Add diced carrot, shallots, pancetta, tomatoes, and garlic, and cook over low heat, stirring occasionally, for 12 to 15 minutes, or until vegetables are soft but not brown. Add lentils, bouquet garni, and 475 ml (16 fl oz) water. Bring to the boil over high heat and skim. Reduce heat to medium, cover, and simmer for about 30 minutes or until lentils are tender. Add 15 ml (1 tsp) salt halfway through cooking time. Drain lentils, discard bouquet garni, and season to taste with additional salt and pepper.

Blanch cabbage leaves in a large pot of boiling, salted water for about 4 minutes or until tender. Drain, refresh under cold water, and drain again. Pat dry with kitchen towels.

Spread cabbage leaves on a work surface and divide lentil mixture among them. Fold cabbage leaves over lentils to form neat parcels.

To serve: Re-warm cabbage parcels in a large steamer for about 5 minutes or until heated through. Re-heat duck and vegetables, if necessary. Place a cabbage parcel on each plate, along with a duck leg and a portion of vegetables. Serve immediately.

Makes 6 servings

Ed. note: The duck legs called for in this recipe can be ordered from D'Artagnan, Inc., 399-419 St. Paul Avenue, Jersey City, New Jersey 07306, (201) 792-0748.

FEUILLANTINE AU CHOCOLAT
CHOCOLATE MOUSSE SQUARES

CHOCOLATE MOUSSE:
75	g (3 oz)	unsalted butter
40	g (1½ oz)	plain chocolate
25	g (1 oz)	plain cocoa powder
2		egg yolks
50	g (2 oz)	sugar
30	ml (2 tbsp)	strong brewed coffee
30	ml (2 tbsp)	water
100	g (4 oz)	double cream, whipped until firm

CHOCOLATE SQUARES:
65	g (2½ oz)	plain chocolate

Prepare chocolate mousse: In a double boiler, combine butter, chocolate, and cocoa; heat until thoroughly melted. Mix well to combine.

Meanwhile, with an electric mixer, whisk egg yolks and sugar until pale and thick. Whisk in coffee and water, then beat in hot chocolate mixture. Turn the mixer on high speed and whisk in whipped cream. Cover and refrigerate for at least 2 hours.

Prepare chocolate squares: In a double boiler, melt 65 g (2½ oz) chocolate. Remove from heat and let cool slightly.

Place a sheet of greaseproof paper on a baking tray and weight down ends of paper securely. Draw a 20 x 25 cm (8 x 10 inch) rectangle.

Pour melted chocolate into centre of rectangle and use a palette knife to spread it as evenly as possible, following the outline you have drawn. Set aside in a cool place to harden; do not refrigerate. When chocolate is nearly firm, use a sharp knife to score 12 rectangles of equal size. Let chocolate harden completely.

Carefully peel chocolate rectangles from greaseproof paper. Place a chocolate rectangle on each plate, top with a large dollop of chocolate mousse, and cover with remaining rectangles.

Makes 6 servings

Ed. note: Use the best plain chocolate you can find for this dessert.

131

Overleaf: Chocolate mousse squares from Michel Trama.

Jacques Maximin

FLEURS DE COURGETTE AUX TRUFFES

STUFFED COURGETTE BLOSSOMS WITH TRUFFLES AND FRESH HERBS

3½	slices white bread, crusts removed
225	ml (8 fl oz) double cream
16	courgettes with blossoms attached
50	ml (2 fl oz) extra virgin olive oil
10	large, fresh basil leaves
1	egg, size 2
	Salt and freshly ground pepper
100	ml (4 fl oz) water
150	g (5 oz) cold unsalted butter
1	40 g (1½ oz) fresh truffle, skinned and thinly sliced
5	ml (1 tsp) truffle juice, optional
100	ml (4 fl oz) crème fraîche, whipped until stiff
25	g (1 oz) fresh chervil leaves
25	g (1 oz) fresh tarragon leaves

In a medium bowl, soak bread in double cream; set aside. Leaving blossoms intact, trim courgettes to 10 cm (4 inch) lengths. Finely chop trimmings. In a small pan, heat 10 ml (2 tsp) olive oil. Add courgette trimmings and sauté over medium-high heat, stirring, for about 2 minutes or until tender. In a blender, combine courgette trimmings, basil leaves, egg, and soaked bread; purée until smooth. Scrape mixture into a bowl, cover, and refrigerate.

136

Heat oven to 200C (400F) gas 6.

Open courgette blossoms very gently and remove centres; try to avoid tearing. Fill a large bowl with cold water and a few ice cubes. Bring a large saucepan of salted water to the boil, add courgettes, and blanch for 10 seconds. Drain and immediately place in iced water. Drain courgettes and blot dry with kitchen paper. With a small kitchen knife, carefully cut courgettes lengthways into 1 cm (½ inch) thick slices; do not cut through blossoms.

Grease a large baking sheet with 25 ml (1½ tbsp) olive oil. Spoon basil mixture into a piping bag fitted with a very small round nozzle. Carefully open each courgette blossom just enough to insert tip of nozzle, and fill three-quarters full with basil mixture. Twist

flower tips to enclose mixture and place on greased baking sheet. Brush courgettes with remaining olive oil and sprinkle with salt and pepper. Cover with aluminium foil and bake for 30 minutes or until tender when pierced with a fork.

Meanwhile, bring water to the boil in a medium saucepan. Add a pinch of salt and pepper and reduce heat to medium. Whisk in butter, 30 ml (2 tbsp) at a time. Remove from heat and add sliced truffle and truffle juice; set aside to infuse.

To serve: Drain courgettes on kitchen paper and place 4 on each plate; press lightly into a fan-like pattern. With a slotted spoon, remove truffle slices from sauce and scatter over courgettes. Bring sauce to the boil over medium heat and whisk in crème fraîche. Season with salt and pepper to taste and pour sauce over courgettes. Sprinkle with chervil and tarragon and serve immediately.

Makes 4 servings

Michel Trama

TERRINE DE POIREAUX A LA VINAIGRETTE ET JULIENNE DE TRUFFES

LEEK TERRINE WITH VINAIGRETTE AND JULIENNE OF TRUFFLES

LEEK TERRINE:

24	to 30 leeks, washed, trimmed, and cut into approximately 25 cm (10 inch) lengths
	about 5 pints water
	Salt and freshly ground pepper

JULIENNE OF TRUFFLES:

2	fresh or preserved truffles, about 40 g (1½ oz)

TRUFFLE VINAIGRETTE:

	Reserved truffle skins
	Juice of 1½ lemons
1.25	ml (¼ tsp) salt
	Pinch freshly ground pepper
225	ml (8 fl oz) safflower or vegetable oil
50	ml (2 fl oz) boiling water

Preceding pages: Jacques Maximin is credited with being the first to use courgettes blossoms in nouvelle cuisine. Here he stuffs them and serves them with fresh herbs.

Prepare leek terrine: Divide leeks into bunches of 6 and tie each with kitchen string.

In a large enamel or stainless-steel saucepan, bring water and 15 ml (1 tbsp) salt to the boil. Add leeks; return to the boil and cook for 10 to 15 minutes. Transfer leeks to a large bowl of iced water to cool. Then drain, squeeze out any excess water, and untie bunches.

Line a 25 x 10 x 7.5 cm (10 x 4 x 3 inch) terrine mould with aluminium foil, leaving a 4 cm (1½ inch) overhang on all sides. Place a layer of about 4 to 5 leeks in bottom of terrine, with white parts at one end. Season with salt and pepper. Layer more leeks on top; this time, the white ends should rest on the green tops of the preceding layer. Repeat alternate layering, seasoning each layer with salt and pepper, until terrine is full. Fold overlapping aluminium foil to cover leeks.

Place a board the size of the interior of the mould on top of leeks. Invert mould, with board in place, on to a dish and place a weight on top of terrine. Refrigerate for at least 6 hours. This will compress the leeks and extract excess water.

Prepare julienne of truffles: With a small kitchen knife, skin truffles and reserve skin for truffle vinaigrette. Slice truffles 3mm (⅛ inch) thick, then cut into 2.5-4 cm (1-1½ inch) strips.

Prepare truffle vinaigrette: In a blender or food processor fitted with a metal blade, process truffle skins, lemon juice, salt, and pepper. Add oil and process to form an emulsion. Add water and process for 1 second longer.

To serve: Remove aluminium-foil-wrapped leeks from terrine; unwrap and invert on to a cutting board. With a large, sharp knife, slice terrine. Spoon truffle vinaigrette over each slice and garnish with julienne of truffles.

Makes 6 servings

Michel Trama layers cooked leeks—white bases on green tops—in a terrine and serves slices chilled.

Jean-Marie Amat

SALADE D'HUITRES AU CAVIAR

SPINACH-WRAPPED OYSTERS
WITH BLACK CAVIAR

24	large fresh spinach leaves
24	fresh oysters, preferably Belon
45	ml (3 tbsp) vinaigrette
2	small shallots, very finely chopped
90	g (3½ oz) black caviar
½	lemon

Blanch spinach leaves in a large pot of boiling salted water for 10 seconds; refresh under cold running water and drain well.

Heat oven to 180C (350F) gas 4.

Shuck oysters and place in a medium saucepan with their liquor. Place the saucepan over medium heat and warm the oysters for about 5 minutes or until their edges begin to curl. With a slotted spoon, transfer oysters to a bowl of cold water to cool; drain well.

Wrap each oyster in a spinach leaf and place in a small baking dish. Stir 15 ml (1 tbsp) of oyster liquor into the vinaigrette and spoon this sauce over the oysters. Sprinkle with shallots. Warm oysters in the oven with the door open for about 1 minute.

Arrange 6 spinach-wrapped oysters on each plate. Top each one with a bit of sauce. Place a small spoonful of caviar on each oyster and top with a drop of lemon juice. Serve immediately.

Makes 4 servings

Jean-Marie Amat recommends fresh Belon oysters for this dish.

André and Arnaud Daguin

LA CHARTREUSE DE PERDREAU

CHARTREUSE OF YOUNG PARTRIDGE

1	small green cabbage, quartered through core so llyves remain intact
225	g (8 oz) fresh, lightly salted, unsmoked bacon, in one piece
15	ml (1 tbsp) plus 10 ml (2 tsp) goose fat
1	onion, finely chopped
1	leek, washed, trimmed, and finely chopped
1	carrot, finely chopped, plus 1 carrot, peeled
475	ml (16 fl oz) chicken stock
1	andouillette sausage or seasoned pork sausage, poached and sliced as thinly as possible
100	g (4 oz) black pudding, poached and sliced as thinly as possible
350	-450 g (12 oz-1 lb) young partridge, cleaned and cut in half lengthways
15	ml (1 tbsp) butter

The Daguins' chartreuse of young partridge.

Heat oven to 140C (275F) gas 1. Blanch cabbage in boiling salted water for about 2 minutes. With a slotted spoon, transfer cabbage to a plate and reserve. With a sharp knife, remove bacon rind, then cut two thin, lengthways slices and reserve. Finely chop remaining bacon.

In a heavy roasting tin, melt 10 ml (2 tsp) goose fat over medium heat. Add chopped bacon, onion, leek, and chopped carrot and sauté for about 5 minutes or until rich brown in colour. Place 4 sections of cabbage on top and add chicken stock; it should cover about half of cabbage. Bring to the boil. Remove from heat and transfer to heated oven. Cook, covered, for 2 to 3 hours. (The longer the cabbage braises, the more flavour it will add to the dish.)

Meanwhile, butter 2 small stainless-steel or oven-proof bowls, 15 cm (6 inches) in diameter and 6-7.5 cm (2½-3 inches) deep. Place a slice of reserved bacon across bottom and extending up sides of each bowl. With a lemon zester, make channels in sides of peeled carrot. Thinly slice carrot and blanch in boiling, salted water for about 3 minutes. Remove with a slotted spoon and line bottom of bowls with carrot slices, covering bacon, if necessary. Line bowls, layering over carrots, with andouillette and black pudding slices. Refrigerate.

Remove cabbage from roasting tin and increase oven temperature to 190C (375F) gas 2. Strain cooking juices into a small bowl; press liquid from braised cabbage and reserve.

In a heavy frying pan heat 30 ml (1 tbsp) goose fat over medium to medium-high heat. Add partridge halves and cook for about 5 minutes or until browned on both sides. Remove partridge and add reserved braising liquid to pan. Cook over medium to high heat until reduced to 100 ml (4 fl oz). Reserve.

Place a layer of cabbage in each prepared bowl and then add half a partridge, skin side down. Add a second layer of cabbage, covering partridge and reaching top of bowls. Cover tightly with aluminium foil and bake in heated oven for 20 minutes.

Remove from oven, uncover, and pour off any excess liquid. To unmould, invert on to a serving dish. Coat with reduced braising liquid and serve.

Makes 2 servings

With a larding needle, thread strips of lard throughout hare fillets. In a frying pan, heat 30 ml (2 tbsp) oil and 45 ml (3 tbsp) butter. Add reserved bones and brown. Add shallots, carrot, celery, thyme, and bay leaf. Continue to cook over medium heat for about 5 minutes or until vegetables soften and colour slightly. Add wine and cook over medium to high heat until reduced to about 225 ml (8 fl oz) of jelly-like glaze. Add stock and boil until reduced to about 225 ml (8 fl oz); strain and reserve. (You should have about 225 ml (8 fl oz) strained liquid.)

In a heavy enamel or stainless-steel saucepan, combine sugar and water. Cook over medium heat until thick, syrupy, and barely coloured. Glaze clementine segments with syrup and reserve.

In a bowl, toss noodles and apples. In a heavy frying pan, heat 30 ml (2 tbsp) butter. Add noodle mixture and cook over low to medium heat until mixture is lightly browned and resembles a pancake. Keep warm and reserve.

In a heavy frying pan, heat 60 ml (4 tbsp) butter and 30 ml (2 tbsp) oil. Add hare fillets and sauté over high heat for 5 to 8 minutes or until browned on all sides, but still rare. Transfer meat to a chopping board and degrease pan. Add reserved wine-stock mixture and deglaze. With pan over low heat, whisk in 45 ml (3 tbsp) butter; do not let sauce boil.

To serve: With a sharp knife, slice fillets lengthways. Spoon a little sauce on to each of 4 heated plates and arrange meat on top. Divide noodle pancake into 4 portions and place one in centre of each plate. Decorate with glazed clementines.

Makes 4 servings

146

Didier Clement

MI-FIGUE MI-RAISIN AU LAIT D'AMANDES

FIGS AND GRAPES
WITH ALMOND ICE CREAM

ALMOND MILK:
    50 g (2 oz) marzipan
   175 ml (6 fl oz) boiled and slightly cooled water
ALMOND ICE CREAM:
     6 egg yolks, size 2
   475 ml (16 fl oz) milk
    50 g (2 oz) sugar
   225 ml (8 fl oz) almond milk
FIGS:
   900 g (2 lb) sugar
   900 ml (1½ pints) water
    16 fresh figs
    16 large Muscat grapes, skinned

Prepare almond milk: In a food processor or blender, process marzipan and water until well combined.

Prepare almond ice cream: In a large bowl, whisk egg yolks for about 1 minute or until light in colour. In a heavy saucepan, combine milk and sugar. Cook over medium heat, stirring with a wooden spoon, just until milk begins to boil. Pour about 100 ml (4 fl oz) hot milk mixture into egg yolks and whisk well. Whisking constantly, pour egg-milk mixture into saucepan and cook over low heat for a few minutes or until mixture thickens enough to coat the back of a spoon. Remove from heat, whisk in almond milk, and set aside to cool completely. Pour cooled mixture into an ice cream machine and freeze according to the manufacturer's directions.

Prepare figs: In a heavy enamel or stainless steel saucepan, heat sugar and water until sugar dissolves. Poach figs in syrup for 4 minutes; remove with a slotted spoon and reserve 12 figs. Purée remaining 4 figs in a blender until smooth; add syrup to thin, if necessary. Strain.

To serve: Coat 4 cold dessert plates with fig purée. Cut off tops of 12 reserved figs and set aside. Arrange 3 figs on each plate and place a small scoop of almond ice cream on each. Place tops of figs on ice cream and decorate plates with grapes.

Makes 4 servings

One way Didier Clément's likes to end a meal: poached figs filled with almond ice cream.

L'ESCALOPE DE FOIE GRAS DE CANARD AUX VIEUX VINAIGRE

SCALLOP OF DUCK FOIE GRAS WITH AGED VINEGAR

MIXED VINEGAR:
- 25 ml (1½ tbsp) aged Bordeaux wine vinegar
- 10 ml (2 tsp) sherry vinegar
- 1.25 ml (¼ tsp) unaged wine vinegar

DUCK FOIE GRAS:
- 350 -450 g (12 oz-1 lb) raw foie gras, cut into four 1 cm (½ inch) thick slices
  Salt and freshly ground pepper
- 50 g (2 oz) plain flour
- 25 ml (1½ tbsp) grapeseed oil, or substitute another mild oil
- 60 ml (4 tbsp) hazelnut oil
- 1 bunch chives, snipped

Prepare mixed vinegar. In a small bowl, combine the Bordeaux wine vinegar, sherry vinegar, and wine vinegar. Set aside.

Prepare foie gras: Sprinkle foie gras with salt and pepper and dush lightly with flour. In a heavy frying pan, heat grapeseed oil. Add foie gras and sauté over medium to high heat for about 3 minutes on each side or until crisp and brown.

Place a slice of foie gras on each of 4 heated serving plates. Baste each piece with 15 ml (1 tbsp) hazelnut oil and 10 ml (2 tsp) mixed vinegar. Sprinkle with snipped chives and serve immediately.

Makes 4 servings

148

ESCALOPE DE TURBOT GRILLEE AUX HUITRES ET AU CAVIAR

GRILLED TURBOT WITH OYSTERS AND CAVIAR

- 750 g (1½ lb) turbot or halibut fillets
- 18 oysters
- 150 ml (¼ pint) Champagne
- 150 ml (¼ pint) crème fraîche
- 100 g (4 oz) cold unsalted butter, cut into pieces
  Salt and freshly ground pepper
- 50 ml (2 fl oz) groundnut oil
  Cayenne pepper
- 25 g (1 oz) Sevruga caviar
- 25 g (1 oz) salmon roe

Rinse fillets and dry well on kitchen towels. Cut fillets into 6 pieces of equal size. If necessary, flatten fish pieces between sheets of moistened greaseproof paper so they are of equal thickness.

Heat grill.

Shuck oysters into a bowl and strain the liquor into a medium saucepan. Add Champagne. Bring to the boil and cook over high heat for about 15 minutes or until reduced by three-quarters. (Note: the sauce will be extremely foamy at first due to the Champagne, so watch carefully.) Whisk in crème fraîche and let sauce return to the boil. Reduce heat to medium and whisk in butter, a few pieces at a time. When all the butter has been incorporated, add oysters and poach over low heat for 5 minutes. Remove from heat.

Season fish on both sides with salt and pepper; lightly brush with groundnut oil. Grill fish, as close to heat as possible, for 2 minutes on each side. Keep warm.

With a slotted spoon, remove oysters from sauce. Re-heat sauce gently, whisking constantly, and season to taste with salt, pepper, and cayenne. Ladle sauce on to 6 plates. Place grilled fish on one side of each plate and arrange 3 oysters on the other side. Divide caviar between plates, spooning it between the oysters. Garnish each plate with salmon roe and serve immediately.

Makes 6 servings

Jean Bardet recommends a simple, elegant foie gras preparation.

Facing page: Gérard Boyer's grilled turbot with oysters and caviar should be served warm with chilled Champagne.

COUNTRY INNS

Chapter

5

OLD-TIME RECIPES AND fresh ingredients: from Périgord to Provence, from Normandy to the Landes, and Auvergne to Gers, for millions of Frenchmen and foreign visitors, real French cooking is not grande cuisine, but fragrant, warming foods like bouillabaisse, boiled pork and cabbage, or a steaming bowlful of tripe. The French are turning back to their regional roots. These dishes are not only nourishing, but are also symbols of the regions that produced them, as evocative of their native soil as landscape, historic buildings, or colourful local customs. A cassoulet, a bourride, or chicken in Bourgueil wine are nothing short of historical monuments that deserve the same protection accorded landmarks.

France is sufficiently rich to number hundreds of men and women, both in modest inns patronized by local farmers or workers and in statelier establishments too, who have become the guardians of a vast and glorious regional heritage that probably numbers ten thousand recipes. Women play a conspicuous and historically important role in preserving these traditions. They learn to cook at their mothers' and grandmothers' knees, then open little restaurants of their own, instead of going on to work in great or well known establishments where for a long time women were not really welcome.

Whether a man or a woman is at the oven, these inns, often (but not always) hidden away in the country, are the best way to discover and grow to love the French heartland. While great restaurants are certainly marvellous, not many provide the warmth and authenticity to be found at Marie-Claude Gracia's, in Poudenas, a village in Gascony with a population of two hundred. Her career began when she and her husband set up a small foie gras canning business, but soon she began thinking of opening a restaurant. She bought an old house in her native village, which she renovated and christened A la Belle Gasconne. Enthusiastic and voluble, Marie-Claude is glad to demonstrate how to cut up a duck, prepare a foie gras, or cook a fish in a casserole with nettles that she has picked along the roadside. Everything at La Belle Gasconne is so pure, so genuine, and so good, from the duck liver terrine to the homemade jams, that you will never want to leave!

A few hundred miles north, in one of the loveliest and best-preserved villages of Normandy, called Beuvron-sur-Auge near Deauville, a fire crackles in the beamed and panelled dining room of Le Pavé d'Auge, situated in the town's sixteenth-century marketplace. Odile Engel, a robust and dynamic woman, is the undisputed queen of Norman cookery, even though she hails from Alsace. So she headed for Normandy, where she fell in love with this village and with all the superb produce available in the region: fish and shellfish that she buys three times a week at the port in Caen, when the little boats come back with their catch of soles, turbots, or John Dory; rabbits, ducks, and pigeons bought at local farms; delicious fresh vegetables and incomparable fresh cream and butter, unlike anything to be found in a supermarket. The Camemberts are rich, unctuous in texture, and delicately flavoured. They have become real museum pieces: you can count on your fingers the number of Norman farmers still making the cheese themselves instead of taking their milk to the plant like everyone else. With such singularly fresh ingredients, Odile Engel turns out mussels in cider, rabbit rillettes, huge sautéed sole, turbot in vinegar, tripe, and chicken in cream like you've never tasted. Most people have probably forgotten such flavours even existed!

France produces some excellent meat but it is very hard to find. Nothing can compare with the rib of beef cooked over vine-cuttings served by Jean-Pierre Xiradakis in La Tupina, a genuine country inn in the middle of Old Bordeaux. Despite his Greek patronymic, Jean-Pierre was born in southwest France. He is a champion of local regional products and has created an association of restaurant owners whose cause it is to promote them.

While scouring the environs to find top-quality ingredients, he discovered near Bazas, southeast of Bordeaux, a very old breed of beef. In the sixteenth century, King Henri IV considered their meat to be the best in the realm. For fifty years, the small-scale production of this beef had steadily declined; the breed might well have disappeared had Jean-Pierre, struck by the remarkable quality of the meat it yielded, not banded together with some local restaurateurs to buy large quantities of meat from the remaining cattle ranchers of Bazas. Production took off again as orders began to pour in from all over France. Since Jean-Pierre is also endowed with an expert nose for sniffing out little-known Bordeaux wines and rare Armagnacs, you are

151

View of the meandering Yonne River.

bound to have a memorable time of it when you visit La Tupina.

Périgord, in the Dordogne, was once upon a time reputed for its excellent female cooks. Nowadays, many of that province's restaurant owners serve identical menus, and these same, monotonous specialties (foie gras, preserved goose, truffles, and cèpe mushrooms) may even come from a jar or a can. Such is absolutely not the case at Solange Gardillou's place. About fifteen years ago, she converted a very old mill, Le Moulin du Roc, into a luxurious inn that stands in a village called Champagnac-de-Bélair. One day, her chef simply vanished; Solange, who had no formal training and cooked as her mother had taught her, had no choice but to take over the kitchen herself. She began to look into old recipes she recalled from her youth, like broiled trout stuffed with cèpe mushrooms. She soon began to invent new combinations of her own, with spectacular results. Simplicity, lightness, and harmony are the keynotes of her highly individual style, which produces such small masterpieces as hot foie gras in a cabbage leaf, herb-stuffed legs of guinea fowl served with a light-textured sauce of foie gras, or her salmon scallop with leeks. The seventeenth-century mill, its machinery intact, has been lovingly embellished; advance reservations are necessary to obtain one of the eleven delightfully decorated rooms, where you will awaken to the sound of birds singing above the river.

At a wild site on the edge of a river, at the foot of cliffs hollowed out with grottoes that were inhabited in prehistoric times, stands a sixteenth-century manor surrounded by flower beds, vegetable gardens, and orchards. This is La Pescalerie, near the village of Cabrerets, twenty miles from Cahors, in the Quercy region. Two doctors, Roger Belcour and Hélène Com-

bette, have restored it in impeccable taste; to earn back some of their investment, they decided to turn the place into a hotel-restaurant. They furnished the house with fine antiques, lovely fabrics, curios, and modern paintings they had collected. Before opening their ten rooms to guests, the owners tried them, one by one, to make sure that a modern traveller would find in them all that might be needed for comfort and well-being.

Hélène comes from an inn-keeping family, and she has managed to amass scores of savoury family recipes that she at first prepared herself. Michel Guérard has since passed on one of his cooks, who is now in charge of the heirloom recipes, though Hélène still keeps an eye on the kitchen. Little do most guests suspect, as they tuck into trout raised in the property's mill stream, the honeyed duck breast, the admirable stuffed cabbage, or the plump and tender farm-raised poultry, the goat cheeses, the succulent desserts, or the wines of Cahors, that the charming, slightly balding gentleman who brings them their food and opens their wine is the head surgeon of the Cahors hospital.

Many French people still buy provisions daily from local greenmarkets.

Facing page: Some markets are open-air; others, like this one in Joigny, are covered. All are central to everyday life in French towns and villages.

152

Unlike Hélène, Roger Belcour has not abandoned his practice; every morning he heads for the hospital in his aged automobile, which he drives back every evening crammed with provisions purchased at the market or at neighbouring farms. When he arrives at La Pescalerie, he pulls on a pair of boots, climbs into a skiff, and hauls in the net that he cast in the river the night before. Afterwards, he hurries to the cellar to bring up a few bottles that he will serve with an appreciative flourish to his customers (somewhat surprised to see the "head waiter" dressed in an old sweater instead of a more formal white jacket).

Every restaurant on the Riviera offers "local fish"—they just don't specify which locality the creatures actually come from. In fact, the fish usually arrive fresh or frozen from the Atlantic coast or even from African shores. During the high season, when the demand is greatest, you can count on the fingers of one hand the number of chefs who manage to procure fish actually caught in the waters between Monte Carlo and Saint Tropez. Adrien and Etienne Sordello are members of that small group. More and more people go to the Restaurant de Bacon in Cap d'Antibes as they would go on a pilgrimage. They are certain to find the freshest, handsomest Mediterranean fish; everyone knows that if only one rock bass remained in the sea, the Sordellos would find it!

If you want to taste a genuine bouillabaisse, visit the Sordellos. Unlike most of their peers, who include only two or three kinds of fish, they make their bouillabaisse with nearly ten varieties, some of which are used just to make the stock. Some people reserve their table a year in advance to be certain they'll have an opportunity to taste this marvellous brew. The restaurant began as a simple wooden hut, and though it has changed somewhat in the last thirty years, it is still a very unpretentious place. If you look up, you may catch a glimpse of Mamma Sordello, who hasn't left her home in fifty years.

Hélène Barale is the queen of Nice's cooks. The restaurant where early in the century her mother prepared Niçois specialties, in addition to selling groceries and coal, has become a kind of municipal monument, filled with hefty farmhouse furniture and kitchen utensils that would

make an antique dealer drool. Too weary these days to serve two meals a day, Hélène opens her doors only in the evening, when she offers her customers a single fixed-price meal.

Niçois cooking is one regional cuisine that has withstood the test of time. In the old centre of Nice are numerous picturesque eateries that perpetuate this venerable culinary tradition. But Hélène's is a must for the best pissaladières (onion, anchovy, and black olive tarts), soccas (a crêpe made with chick-pea flour and olive oil), salade Niçoise (radishes, onions, green peppers, tomatoes, olives, and anchovies), ravioli, and three-meat daubes (stews) that simmer in the oven for three hours and more. Follow that with an extraordinary sweetened seakale tart with apricot jam, coffee, and an old Marc de Provence (grape brandy); if she feels up to it, Hélène may crank up one of her player pianos, and even sing along, just like in her *maman*'s day.

At Chez Fifine in Saint Tropez, if you take care to order in advance, you can indulge in the world's best aioli. About twenty miles away is Bormes-les-Mimosas where the Gedda brothers reign. They are past masters at Provençal cuisine, in their rose-covered restaurant La Tonnelle des Délices.

Edith Remoissent will serve as the grand finale. She lives in a tiny village, Vignoles, just outside Beaune in Burgundy. She is young, attractive, lively, and whimsical. In her vine-covered cottage nestled in the shadow of the church steeple, she has set up large farmhouse tables, benches, a few chairs, and when she reaches her limit of twenty guests, she hangs up a sign that reads "Full." You will be seated amidst jam pots, jars of pickles, huge loaves of bread; beyond the window, you can watch the pet cats and dogs chase chickens in the long grass.

Edith learned to cook on her own; indeed, nothing is less like a typical restaurant than Au Petit Truc. No one gets past the door without a reservation, even if the dining room is half empty. And what glorious food! The finest, most authentic, and heart-warming kind of country cooking, rendered with rare imagination and subtlety. Nowhere else will you find an aspic of young rabbit with chervil, an old-fashioned crayfish terrine (a dish that dates from the seventeenth century), a veal terrine with Chablis, or snails with potatoes au gratin to compare with Edith's. Nor so sublime a chocolate tart, made from a jealously guarded secret recipe that Edith swears she will reveal only to the man she marries!

Each day, Hélène Barale offers a single menu of Niçois cooking that reflects the farmer's season and the fisherman's catch.

Facing page: Fishing boats at Cannes, on the French Riviera.

BISTRO CUISINE

THE WORD "BISTRO" IS UN-translatable, but it is understood the world over. It is an evocative term that summons up images of brownish walls shiny with age, oilcloth on the tables, a zinc-covered bar tended by the owner in shirt-sleeves, who serves up Beaujolais and Côtes-du-Rhône, robust waitresses who joke with the regulars, and the aroma of rabbit stewed with tomatoes and mushrooms or lamb ragoût simmering on the back burner in a kitchen not much bigger than a broom closet.

Along with berets and long loaves of French bread, bistros deserve a place of honour on the French coat of arms. Strangely, the word is not French at all. "Bistro" supposedly dates from the arrival of Russian occupation troops who in 1815 camped out on the Champs-Elysées after Napoleon's defeat at Waterloo. Very thirsty and pressed for time, the czar's soldiers are said to have crowded into the city's cafés crying, "Bystro! bystro!" (that is, "Quick! quick!").

Russian origin or not, the bistro is as much a part of our national heritage as Notre Dame, the Louvre, or the Eiffel Tower. It is a peculiarly Parisian phenomenon, although it has equivalents in all the cities and towns of France. In Lyons, for instance, they are called *bouchons* or *machons*, from the name of the traditional meal based on salted or cured meats (charcuterie) served between 10 and 11 a.m. in these small, always picturesque spots. In Strasbourg, bistros are called "winstubs" (wine bars). They are extremely popular institutions, where a mixed crowd of young and old, rich and less rich, meet in rooms panelled in dark wood, to taste the newest vintage, tuck into hearty dishes cooked by the owner's wife, and laugh and joke in a warm, merry atmosphere.

Traditionally, bistros have been family businesses: Mama or Papa works at the oven, and the staff is solidly entrenched. It is too soon to say that bistros are relics of the past, but it is certain that these little restaurants are seriously threatened by the encroachment of fast-food chains, snack bars, and other forms of eating on the run. Some bistros now have the food they serve delivered from centralized kitchens, where it has been vacuum-packed; although no one wants to admit it, it appears that this system is increasingly widespread. It has become more important than ever to know just where you are eating and how to tell a genuine bistro from the ersatz.

Bistro cuisine is really nothing more or less than the kind of cooking that has always been

At s'Burjerstuewel—a winstub that regular customers call "Chez Yvonne"—in Strasbourg, strangers and friends alike partake of hearty specialties and local wines.

growths are listed beside lesser-known but choice bottles selected for their quality and their personality is considered more impressive, so sommeliers need a broader range of expertise. Many make frequent trips to the wine regions and attend comparative wine tastings.

This new breed is an elite, of course, and the stars are Marcel Périnet (Georges Blanc, in Vonnas), George Pertuiset (Lameloise, in Chagny), Werner Heil (Gerard Boyer, in Reims), Jean-Claude Jambon (Faugeron, in Paris), Marc Brockart (Apicius, in Paris), Antoine Hernandez (Robuchon, in Paris), Jean-Claude Maître (Le Crillon, Paris), Jean-Pierre Rous (Le Royal-Gray, Cannes), Jean Jacques (Bardet, in Châteauroux), Jacques Mélac (42 rue Leon Frot, Paris), Jean-Luc Pouteau (Le Pavillon de l'Elysée, Paris). The latter won the title of "World's Best Sommelier" in Brussels. There are others, of course, too numerous to name.

Wine madness has seized a growing number of chefs and restaurateurs. Many of them play the role of sommelier themselves, purchasing their own wine at the vineyards, taking courses in oenology, participating in blind tastings. Some of them have become leading wine experts. Although some restaurants offer less than the best vintages of the best wines, all the fine establishments in this book, and most other restaurants, regard wine as an object of fervent interest. A case in point was the late, much lamented Jean Troisgros, who was pretty nearly unbeatable in blind tastings; other illustrious ones are Alain Chapel, Jacques Pic, Pierre Laporte, Michel Guérard, Marc Meneau, Jean-Claude Vrinat, Alain Dutournier, Guy Savoy, Michel Oliver, Alain Senderens, Lucien Vanel, Michel Trama, Christian Clément, Jean-Marie Amat, Pierre Menneveau (at Rôtisserie du Chambertin, in Gevrey-Chambertin), and doz-

ens of others. Women are not yet very numerous, but often prove to have exceptional flair, as in the cases of Jacqueline Lorain (in Joigny), Sophie Bardet (in Châteauroux), Madame Barrat (Le Lion d'Or, in Romorantin), or Maryse Allarousse (Le Panorama, in Dardilly, near Lyon), who even captured the title "Best Sommelière in France."

Of all the pleasures of the table, wine arouses the most curiosity. It has its own special lore, not necessarily rational, which has been handed down from generation to generation. But because gastronomy, including the choice of a wine, is ideally an art of nuance, only your own experience and pleasure should determine your likes and dislikes. All of the once-inviolable laws have in fact been questioned during the past twenty years, and as many have been found wrong-headed as have been justified. People are more open-minded, trying unexpected combinations of wine and food. Some, like Sophie Bardet or Alain Senderens, have gone so far as to compose meals around wines, instead of vice versa.

164

Bordeaux, France's most important wine region, has thirty-thousand vineyards. Despite family resemblances and characteristics, no two vintages of the same wine are identical.

It is an interesting experiment to try yourself; if you have some favourite wines, consider asking the restaurant owner in advance to compose a meal around them. It may well be one of the greatest gustatory pleasures of your life.

Even without going quite so far, it is worthwhile to keep some unconventional but exciting possibilities in mind. Here are a few ideas.

1. It is not true that mixing red and white wines brings on headaches; headaches result from over-indulgence. A thoughtful combination of white and red wines can create harmonies and contrasts that you would miss if you limited yourself to a single wine.

2. It is not necessarily true that an older wine should be decanted. Prolonged contact with air often "kills" the wine. In a test with two bottles of Lafite-Rothschild 1870, one was opened two hours before the meal and decanted into a carafe; it lost a great deal of its aroma. The second bottle, uncorked at the last moment, had all its bouquet intact. However, a young or slightly hard red wine may gain from being decanted, for the

contact with oxygen will soften it a bit.

3. The practice of bringing red wine to room temperature was justified when houses were chilly and the wine was brought directly from the cellar where the temperature hovered around 12C (53F). Today, houses and flats are generally well heated, and it is absurd to bring a Bordeaux or Burgundy to a room temperature of 20C (68F) because the wine becomes heavy and unpleasant to drink. To appreciate a good red wine, it should not be warmer than about 17C (63F) for a claret, 14C (58F) for a red Burgundy. But a too-low temperature can kill some wines. A Beaujolais served in an ice-bucket will not release its bouquet, and a white Burgundy or Côtes-du-Rhône will be far better at 12C (54F) than if served icy cold. An Alsatian wine, or a Loire Valley white will be perfect at about 10.5C (51F). And as a general rule, a young, or "hard," red wine will improve if served cold, for its fruit will be more apparent.

4. It is a mistake to serve too many great wines at one meal. A great opera production rarely has a half-dozen divas! One or two are more than sufficient: that way, instead of competing they can complement each other.

5. Memorable meals can centre around modest wines, as long as they have been chosen with care. There are innumerable appealing little wines like Saint-Véran (Burgundy), Chinon (Loire), Cornas (Côtes-du-Rhône), Bandol (Provence), Bergerac (southwest), and many others that can harmonize nicely.

Here are some suggestions for marrying wines with food.

Foie gras: Sauternes is fine, but other white wines would go well too, like a Meursault or Montrachet from Burgundy, an Alsatian Tokay or Gewürztraminer, a Savennières from the Loire, or a Condrieu, Hermitage, or Château-

165

Regardless of the colour of the skin, the juice of red wine grapes is colourless. The final red colour comes from fermenting the juice with the skins and pips, which are eventually removed.

neuf-du-Pape from the Côtes-du-Rhône; or you could try a Beaumes-de-Venise from that area, which is a bit like Sauternes, only less sweet. Certain red wines are agreeable accompaniments too: rustic wines like Cahors and Bergerac, or even a Bordeaux Cru Bourgeois.

If you have it at the end of the meal, just before the cheese, foie gras pairs off beautifully with an old red or white port, or even a Sherry that you can continue to drink with some Roquefort cheese.

Oysters and Shellfish: Muscadet is often recommended, and a good one such as Metaireau's is fine. But Muscadet is often too acid, so you might prefer a dry white Graves, a Sancerre, a Chablis, or even a big, tasty Bourgogne like Corton-Charlemagne. Don't neglect young reds that may be drunk chilled, like Chinon, Bandol, Coteaux d'Aix-en-Provence, or an Alsatian Pinot Noir. They all go well with the iodine flavour of oysters.

Crustaceans: With cold lobster, crab, or prawns choose a dry white wine with some fruitiness, like a Sancerre, a Quincy, a Saint Pour-

çain, or a Riesling. If they are served hot, crustaceans marry well with nobler, softer wines: Pouilly-Fuissé, Meursault, Puligny-Montrachet (all Burgundies), Coulée de Serrant (Anjou), Hermitage, Saint-Joseph, or Condrieu (Côtes-du-Rhône).

Fish: With fish in a butter sauce, try white wines from the Loire (Saumur, Sancerre, Pouilly-Fumé). With red wine sauces, drink the same red wine, or else a fat white wine from Burgundy or the Côtes-du-Rhône, which will contrast with the sauce, yet not overwhelm it. If you are having smoked salmon or caviar, red wine is disastrous. But with fresh grilled salmon accompanied by a sauce Béarnaise, or even with a grilled sole, a cool red wine (Bordeaux, Loire, Beaujolais, or Bouzy from Champagne) would be just the ticket. With little fried fish, Muscat d'Alsace is lovely; with bouillabaisse, try a white wine from Provence.

Lamb: With milk-fed lamb, the best choice would be a medium-bodied red (Pauillac, Saint-Estèphe, Saint-Julien). With a leg or saddle of lamb, a great Bordeaux or a good Provençal

166

The French grape harvest begins in late September or early October.

wine (Côtes d'Aix, Bandol). With lamb or mutton in a sauce, choose a red from the Loire (Saumur-Champigny, Bourgueil), a Côtes-du-Rhône (Gigondas), or a wine from Languedoc (Fitou, Corbières).

Beef: If it's a grilled cut, any simple red wine will do (Beaujolais, Languedoc, Côtes-du-Rhône Villages, a modest Bordeaux). If the meat is of exceptional quality, pick something a cut above. With an excellent beef rib grilled over vine cuttings the way they do in Bordeaux, there's no reason not to select a superb Médoc, or even a prestigious Pomerol. In Normandy, I once was served a glass of Calvados with my beef. After a moment of hesitation, I took a sip: fantastic. Pot-au-feu takes a rustic red wine (Morgon, Cahors, Côtes de Buzet, Bergerac, Chinon), and with boeuf bourguignon, choose a relatively simple Burgundy, like a Rully, a Passe-tout-grain, or a Mercurey.

Pork: With charcuterie, a cool Gamay, a Beaujolais, or else a dry white Vouvray. Cooked, pork is generally a rich or even fatty meat, and requires a fresh young red, served cool, like a

Château Monbazillac is the estate of Bergerac's most well known wine, a rich, white dessert wine resembling Sauternes.

Beaujolais, Pinot Noir d'Alsace, a Cahors, or a Bergerac. These same wines are fine with choucroute (sauerkraut), which need not always be accompanied by a white Alsatian wine.

Chicken: There's nothing better with broiled chicken than a young red wine from the Côtes de Beaune (Savigny, Blagny), the Médoc, or the Loire (Champigny, Bourgueil). If the chicken is prepared in a cream sauce, try a white Burgundy (Meursault) or a light red, say a Beaujolais.

The individuality of a wine starts with the grapes, the soil, and the climate.

Duck: This fowl calls for sturdy, structured wines: a great Medoc, a Pomerol, a Hermitage; but don't overlook less prestigious wines like Cahors, Madiran, or a Saint-Joseph from the Côtes-du-Rhône.

Game: White-fleshed game (pheasant or partridge) goes very well with light red Burgundies (Chambolle-Musigny, Clos de Vougeot), but do try a roast young partridge with a white Burgundy such as Bâtard-Montrachet; you are sure to be agreeably surprised. Dark-fleshed game (venison, hare, boar) calls for rich and powerful red wines: Gevrey-Chambertin, Pommard (Burgundies), Châteauneuf-du-Pape, Côte Rôtie, Hermitage (Côtes-du-Rhône), or a great Pomerol. But certain sweet white wines (Sauternes, Anjou), or an old Tokay d'Alsace, or even a great old white Burgundy (Corton-Charlemagne) can complement the rich taste of game in sauce.

Cheeses: Red wines are not the only ones that should be drunk with a Brie, Roquefort, or farm-cured Camembert. A strong cheese kills a great wine, so the best choice is a robust, tannic red wine, like red Sancerre, Côtes-du-Rhône Villages, Bergerac, Cahors, or Madiran. Certain white wines make good partners for some cheeses, for example Sauternes with Roquefort, white Hermitage with Saint-Nectaire, Riesling with Munster or Livarot, wines from Savoie with Gruyère or Tomme, and Sancerre with goat cheeses.

Desserts: It is notoriously difficult to choose a wine to end the meal, since desserts containing alcohol or based on fruit do not go well with wine. In a pinch, you can serve a light red or white (Anjou, Saumur, Bourgueil, Sancerre) with a fruit tart, and with pastries, a dry white Graves. A Muscat de Beaumes-de-Venise or an old white Banyuls (a naturally sweet wine from the Eastern Pyrénées, aged in barrels set out in the sun) are marvellous with chocolate desserts. Another unusual but delicious match is medium-dry Sherry with fruit sorbets. Another quite suitable solution is to end the meal with the white or red wine that accompanied the preceding course.

And why not try Champagne? Sixty percent of the Champagne consumed in France is drunk with dessert. Try a pink Champagne. Its solid structure goes admirably with the sweet flavours of desserts.

APPENDIXES

I BORDEAUX AND BURGUNDY VINTAGES

Just like a living being, wine evolves, improves, or deteriorates with time. As it ages, a mediocre vintage may turn out to be a winner. Unfortunately, the reverse is also true. What follows is an overview of the last several vintages in Bordeaux and Burgundy.

EXCEPTIONAL YEAR	*****
VERY GREAT YEAR	****
GREAT YEAR	***
GOOD YEAR	**
MEDIOCRE YEAR	*
POOR YEAR	-

BORDEAUX

Year		Rating	Year		Rating
1984	Reds	*	1978	Reds	****
	Whites	**		Whites	-
1983	Reds	****	1977	Reds	-
	Whites	***		Whites	-
1982	Reds	*****	1976	Reds	**
	Whites	**		Whites	**
1981	Reds	****	1975	Reds	*
	Whites	**		Whites	***
1980	Reds	**	1970	Reds	****
	Whites	*		Whites	***
1979	Reds	***			
	Whites	*			

BURGUNDIES

Year		Rating	Year		Rating
1984	Reds	*	1978	Reds	****
	Whites	**		Whites	*
1983	Reds	**	1976	Reds	****
	Whites	***		Whites	****
1982	Reds	**			
	Whites	****			
1981	Reds	*			
	Whites	*			
1980	Reds	-			
	Whites	-			
1979	Reds	**			
	Whites	***			

The most famous sparkling wines in the world are produced in northeastern France, near Reims, where the kings of France were once crowned. The process that cultivates the bubbles in fine Champagne takes six or seven years, during which time a bottle may be handled two hundred times.

Since 1855 the red wine of Bordeaux has been divided into five categories of "growths." Recently, Gault-Millau magazine conducted a survey in which three hundred specialists (oenologists, brokers, sommeliers, wine merchants) were questioned in an attempt to establish a hierarchy of the best red clarets. What follows are lists of our specialists' favourites, in the order of preference on a scale of 1 to 100.

Premièrs Crus (First growths)		Deuxièmes Crus (Second growths)	
Latour	98	Ducru-Beaucaillou	96
Margaux	90	Pichon-Longueville,	
Haut-Brion	90	Comtesse de Lalande	96
Mouton-Rothschild	88	Léoville-Las Cases	95
Lafite-Rothschild	85	Cos d'Estournel	89
		Gruaud-Larose	71

Troisièmes Crus (Third growths)		Cinquièmes Crus (Fifth growths)	
Palmer	97	Lynch-Bages	100
Giscours	95	Grand-Puy-Lacoste	100
La Lagune	94	Haut-Batailley	100
Calon-Ségur	89	Dauzac	98
		Cantemerle	96
Quatrièmes Crus (Fourth growths)		Clerc-Milon	96
		Pontet-Canet	94
Prieuré-Lichine	91	Mouton-Baronne-	
Talbot	89	Philippe	93
Duhart-Milon-		Batailley	91
Rothschild	88		
Beychevelle	84		

Although they are less renowned, the Cru Bourgeois of the Médoc are very fashionable right now; they are excellent buys. Our jury of specialists singled out the following wines as particularly worthy of note:

Chasse-Spleen, Gloria, de Pez, Sociando-Mallet, Phelan-Ségur, Meyney, Poujeaux-Theil, Haut-Marbuzet, Siran, Bel-Air-Marquis d'Aligre, Lanessan.

The official classification of 1855 included only one wine from the Graves region: Haut-Brion. This state of affairs ought to be righted; here are some of today's best wines from Graves:

La Mission-Haut-Brion, Domaine de Chevalier, Haut-Bailly, Pape-Clément, Smith-Haut-Lafitte, Fieuzal, Carbonnieux, Bouscaut, Olivier.

The red wines of Pomerol are not subject to any classification, although they are among the best wines of Bordeaux. They often command higher prices than the most well known Médocs. Herewith, a short list of the "stars" of Pomerol in the order of my personal preference:

Petrus, Trotanoy, L'Evangile, Lafleur-Petrus, La Conseillante, Petit-Village, Latour-Pomerol, Vieux-Château-Certan, Certan de May, Lagrange, Nenin, Gazin, L'Eglise, L'Eglise-Clinet, Clos René, La Pointe, Le Bon Pasteur, Beauregard.

The red wines of Saint-Emilion are innumerable and have their own classification system. The following are some of the most highly regarded:

Cheval Blanc, Figeac, Ausone, L'Angélus, La Gaffelière, Pavie, Balestard-la-Tonnelle, Corbin-Michotte, Grand-Barrail-Lamarzelle-Figeac, Grand-Mayne, Grand-Corbin, La Dominique, Saint-Georges, Soutard, Grâce-Dieu.

And finally, Sauternes, considered to be the best sweet white wines on earth:

d'Yquem, Suduiraut, Coutet, Climens, Guiraud, Lafaurie-Peyraguey, Rieussec, Filhot, de Malle, de Rayne-Vigneau, Haut-Peyraguey, La Tour-Blanche, Gilette.

III RESTAURANT ADDRESSES

PARIS

1st arrondissement

Le Carré des Feuillants
14 rue de Castiglione
42.96.67.92.
Service until 10:30 pm.
Closed Saturday and Sunday.
Card: V.

Le Grand Véfour
17 rue de Beaujolais
42.96.56.27.
Service until 10:15 pm.
Closed Saturday,
Sunday; August.
Cards: V, AE, DC.

Lescure
7 rue de Mondovi
42.60.18.91.
Service until 10 pm.
Closed Saturday
evening and Sunday.

Vendome (Hôtel Ritz)
15 place Vendôme
42.60.38.30.
Open daily.
Cards: V, AE, DC, EC.

3rd arrondissement

L'Ambassade d'Auvergne
22 rue du Grenier-
Saint-Lazare
42.72.31.22.
Service until 1 am.
Closed Sunday.
Cards: V.

L'Ami Louis
32 rue du Vertbois
48.87.77.48.
Service until 10:30 pm.
Closed Monday, Tuesday;
July 1–September 30.
Cards: V, AE, DC.

4th arrondissement

Benoît
20 rue Saint-Martin
42.72.25.76.
Service until 10 pm.
Closed Saturday,
Sunday; August.

Au Gourmet de l'Isle
42 rue Saint-Louis-en-l'Ile
43.26.79.27.
Service until 9:30 pm.
Closed Monday, Thursday;
July 25–September 1.

Au Pont Marie
7 quai de Bourbon
43.54.79.62.
Service until 10 pm.
Closed Saturday and Sunday.

5th arrondissement

La Tour d'Argent
15–17 quai de la Tournelle
43.54.23.31.
Service until 10 pm.
Closed Monday.
Cards: V, AE, DC.

6th arrondissement

Allard
41 rue Saint-André-dés-Arts
43.26.48.23.
Service until 10:30 pm.
Closed Saturday,
Sunday; August.
Cards: V, DC.

Jacques Cagna
14 rue des
Grands Augustins
43.26.49.39.
Service until 10:30 pm.
Closed Saturday, Sunday;
December 24–
January 2; August.
Cards: V, AE, DC.

Lapérouse
51 quai des
Grands Augustins
43.26.68.04.
Service until 11 pm.
Closed Saturday lunch,
Sunday.
Cards: V, AE, DC, EC.

Le Petit Saint-Benoît
4 rue Saint-Benoît
42.60.27.92.
Service until 10 pm.
Closed Saturday and Sunday.

7th arrondissement

Babkine (Chez Germaine)
30 rue Pierre-Leroux
42.73.28.34.
Service until 9 pm.
Closed Saturday evening,
Sunday; August.

Le Bourdonnais
113 ave. de la Bourdonnais
47.05.47.96.
Service until 11 pm.
Closed Sunday and Monday.
Cards: V, AE, DC.

Le Divellec
107 rue de l'Université
45.51.91.96.
Service until 10 pm.
Closed Sunday, Monday;
December 24–January 2;
August 2–September 2.
Cards: V, AE, DC.

La Fontaine de Mars
129 rue Saint-Dominique
47.05.46.44.
Service until 9:15 pm.
Closed Saturday evening
and Sunday.

Au Pied de Fouet
45 rue de Babylone
47.05.12.27.
Service until 9 pm.
Closed Saturday evening
and Sunday.

Jules Verne
Eiffel Tower (2nd floor)
45.55.61.44.
Service until 10:30 pm.
Open daily.
Cards: V, AE.

8th arrondissement

Les Ambassadeurs
(Hôtel de Crillon)
10 place de la Concorde
42.65.24.24.
Service until 10:30 pm.
Open daily.
Cards: V, AE, DC.

Laurent
41 ave. Gabriel
47.23.79.18.
Service until 11 pm.
Closed Saturday lunch,
Sunday.
Cards: AE, DC.

Lucas-Carton
9 place de la Madeleine
42.65.22.90.
Service until 10:30 pm.
Closed Saturday, Sunday;
August 2–22.
Card: V.

Maxim's
3 rue Royale
42.65.27.94.
Service until 1 am.
Closed Sunday.
Cards: V, AE, DC.

Pavillon de l'Elysée
10 Champs-Elysées
42.65.85.10.
Service until 11 pm.
Closed Saturday, Sunday;
August 2–31.
Cards: V, AE, DC.

Taillevent
15 rue Lamennais
45.63.39.94.
Service until 10:30 pm.
Closed Saturday, Sunday;
July 26–August 25.

15th arrondissement

Olympe
8 rue Nicolas-Charlet
47.34.86.08.
Service until 12 midnight.
Closed Monday; lunch
(except Thursday);
August 1–22.
Cards: V, AE, DC.

16th arrondissement

Robuchon
32 rue de Longchamp
47.27.12.27.
Service until 10:15 pm.
Closed Saturday, Sunday;
June 30–July 27.
Cards: V, AE, DC.

Guy Savoy
28 rue Duret
45.00.17.67.
Service until 10:30 pm.
Closed Saturday, Sunday.
Card: V.

17th arrondissement

Le Manoir de Paris
6 rue Pierre Demours
45.72.25.25.
Service until 10:30 pm.
Closed Saturday, Sunday;
July 5–August 4.
Cards: V, AE, DC.

Michel Rostang
20 rue Rennequin
47.63.40.77.
Service until 10:15 pm.
Closed Saturday (except
lunch May–September),
Sunday; July 26–August 26.
Card: V.

18th arrondissement

Le Bateau Lavoir
8 rue Garreau
46.06.02.00.
Service until 10 pm.
Open daily.

Le Petit Marguery
8 rue Aristide Bruant
42.64.95.81.
Service until 9:30 pm.
Closed Sunday, Monday; September.

Outside Paris

La Vieille Fontaine
8 ave. Gréty
49.62.01.78.
Service until 10 pm.
Closed Sunday, Monday;
August.
Cards: V, AE, DC.

THE PROVINCES

ALSACE

Auberge de l'Ill
Rue de Collonges
Illhaeusern
68150 Ribeauvillé
89.71.83.23.
Service until 9 pm.
Closed Monday
(evening only in summer),
Tuesday; 1st week of July.
Cards: AE, DC.

Le Crocodile
10 rue de l'Outre
67000 Strasbourg
88.32.13.02.
Service until 10 pm.
Closed Sunday, Monday;
July 8–August 4.
Cards: AE, DC.

BURGUNDY

Georges Blanc
(La mère Blanc)
01540 Vonnas
74.50.00.10.
Service until 9:30 pm.
Cards: V, AE, DC.

La Côte d'Or
2 rue d'Argentine
21210 Saulieu
80.64.07.66.
Service until 10 pm.
Closed Tuesday;
Wednesday lunch
(November 1–March 31,
exc. holidays).
Cards: V, AE, DC.

La Côte Saint-Jacques
14 Faubourg de Paris
89300 Joigny
86.62.09.70.
Service until 9:30 pm.
Cards: V, AE, DC.

L'Espérance
Saint-Père-sous-Vézelay
89450 Vézelay
86.33.20.45.
Service until 9:30 pm.
Closed Tuesday,
Wednesday lunch.
Cards: V, AE.

Lameloise
36 place d'Armes
71150 Chagny
85.87.08.85.
Service until 9:30 pm.
Closed Wednesday evening,
Thursday lunch.
Card: V.

Au Petit Truc
Place de l'Eglise
21200 Beaune
80.22.01.76.
Service until 9 pm.
Closed Monday, Tuesday;
August 3–21.

BRITTANY, NORMANDY

Le Bretagne
13 rue Saint-Michel
56230 Questembert
97.26.11.12.
Service until 9:30 pm.
Closed Sunday evening
(exc. July, August).
Cards: V, AE, DC.

Château de Locguénolé
Route de Port-Louis
56700 Hennebont
97.76.29.04.
Service until 9:30 pm.
Cards: V, AE, DC, EC.

Le Pavé d'Auge
Place du Village
14430 Dozulé
31.79.26.71.
Service until 9 pm.
Closed Tuesday and
Wednesday evenings.
Cards: V, AE.

Restaurant de Bricourt
1 rue Duguesclin
35260 Cancale
99.89.64.76.
Service until 9:30 pm.
Closed Tuesday, Wednesday.
Cards: V, EC.

CHAMPAGNE AND THE NORD

Boyer (Château des Crayères)
64 blvd. Henry-Vasnier
51100 Reims
26.82.80.80.
Service until 9:30 pm.
Closed Monday,
Tuesday lunch.
Cards: V, AE, DC, EC.

Le Flambard
79 rue d'Angleterre
59000 Lille
20.51.00.06.
Service until 9:30 pm.
Closed Sunday evening,
Tuesday; August.
Cards: AE, DC.

RIVIERA

Barale
39 rue Beaumont
06000 Nice
Service until 9 pm.
Closed Saturday.
Dinner only.

Chantecler (Hôtel Negresco)
37 Promenade des Anglais
06000 Nice
93.88.39.51.
Open daily.
Service until 10:30 pm.
Cards: V, AE, DC, EC.

Chez Fifine
5 rue Cépoun-San-Martin
83990 Saint Tropez
94.97.03.90.
Closed Monday; off-season.

Dominique Le Stanc
18 blvd. des Moulins
Monte Carlo
93.50.63.37.
Service until 10 pm.
Closed Sunday, Monday.
Cards: V, AE, DC.

Le Moulin de Mougins
424 chemin du Moulin
Quartier Notre-Dame-de-Vie
06250 Mougins
93.75.78.24.
Service until 10:30 pm.
Closed Monday,
Thursday; lunch.
Cards: V, AE, DC.

L'Oasis
Rue Jean-Honoré-Carle
06210 Mandelieu
93.49.95.52.
Service until 9:30 pm.
Closed Monday evening,
Tuesday.

La Palme d'Or
(Hôtel Martinez)
73 blvd. de la Croisette
06400 Cannes
93.84.10.24.
Service until 11 pm.
Cards: VC, AE, DC, EC.

Restaurant de Bacon
Blvd. de Bacon
06600 Cap d'Antibes
93.61.77.70.
Service until 10 pm.
Closed Sunday evening,
Monday; November 15–
February 1.
Cards: AE, DC.

Le Royal-Gray
(Hôtel Gray d'Albion)
6 rue des Etats-Unis
06400 Cannes
93.48.54.54.
Service until 10 pm.
Closed Sunday evening;
Monday off-season.
Cards: V, AE, DC.

La Terrasse (Hôtel Juana)
Ave. Georges-Gallice
06160 Juan-les-Pins
93.61.20.37.
Service until 10 pm.
Dinner only (July 1–
August 31).
Closed October 20–March 20.

La Tonnelle des Délices
Place Gambetta
83230 Bormes-les-Mimosas
94.71.34.84.
Service until 10 pm.
Closed October 1–March 31.

PROVENCE

L'Oustau de Baumanière
Au Val d'Enfer
13520 Maussane-les-Alpilles
90.97.33.07.
Service until 9:45 pm.
Closed Wednesday, Thursday
lunch.
Cards: V, AE, DC, EC.

LYONS AND THE RHÔNE VALLEY

Paul Bocuse
50 quai de la Plage
69660 Collonges-
au-Mont-d'Or
78.22.01.40.
Service until 9:30 pm.
Cards: V, AE, DC.

Alain Chapel
RN 83
01390 Saint-André-de-Corcy
79.91.82.02.
Service until 10 pm.
Cards: AE, DC.

Pierre Gagnaire
3 rue Georges-Teissier
42000 Saint-Etienne
77.37.57.93.
Service until 9:30 pm.
Closed Sunday, Monday;
August 9–September 9.
Cards: V, AE, DC.

Léon de Lyon
1 rue Pleney
(1st arrondissement)
69000 Lyon
78.28.11.23.
Service until 10 pm.
Closed Monday lunch, Sunday.
Card: V.

Pic
285 ave. Victor-Hugo
26000 Valence
75.44.15.32.
Service until 9:30 pm.
Closed Sunday evening,
Wednesday; August.
Cards: AE, DC.

La Tour Rose
16 rue du Boeuf (5th)
69000 Lyon
78.37.25.90.
Closed Sunday.
Cards: V, AE, DC, EC.

Troisgros
Place de la Gare
42300 Roanne
77.71.66.97.
Service until 9:30 pm.
Closed Tuesday,
Wednesday lunch; August
Cards: V, AE, DC.

MASSIF CENTRAL

Lou Mazuc
12210 Laguiole
65.44.32.24.
Service until 9 pm.
Closed Sunday evening;
Monday (exc. July–August).
Card: AE.

LOIRE REGION

Jean Bardet
1 rue J.-J. Rousseau
36000 Châteauroux
54.34.82.69.
Service until 9:30 pm.
Closed Sunday evening;
Monday.
Cards: V, AE, DC, EC.

Le Lion d'Or
69 rue Georges-Clemenceau
41200 Romorantin
54.76.00.28.
Service until 9 pm.
Cards: V, AE, DC, EC.

Le Relais
1 ave. de Chambord
41250 Bracieux
54.46.41.22.
Service until 9 pm.
Closed Tuesday evening,
Wednesday.
Cards: V, AE, DC

PÉRIGORD-QUERCY

Le Moulin du Roc
24530 Champagnac de Bélair
53.54.80.36.
Service until 9:30 pm.
Closed Tuesday,
Wednesday evening.
Cards: V, AE, DC, EC.

La Pescalerie
46330 Cabrerets
65.31.22.55.
Service until 9 pm.
Closed November 1–April 1.
Cards: V, AE, DC.

SOUTHWEST

L'Aubergade
52 rue Royale
47270 Puymirol
53.95.31.46.
Service until 9:30 pm.
Closed Monday (exc. July–
August and holidays).
Cards: V, AE.

A la Belle Gasconne
47170 Mézin
53.65.71.58.
Service until 9:30 pm.
Closed Sunday evening,
Monday; January 16–
February 10, November 1–15.
Cards: V, AE, DC.

Clavel
44 rue Charles-Domercq
33000 Bordeaux
56.92.91.52.
Service until 9:30 pm.
Closed Sunday, Monday;
July 15–31; February
school holidays.
Cards: AE, DC, V.

Dubern
42 allées de Tourny
33000 Bordeaux
56.48.03.44.

Michel Guerard
Eugénie-les-Bains
40320 Geaune
58.51.19.01.
Service until 10 pm.
Closed November 4–March 30.
Card: AE.

Hôtel de France
Place de la Libération
32000 Auch
65.05.00.44.
Service until 9:30 pm.
Closed Sunday evening,
Monday; January.
Cards: V, AE, DC, EC.

Les Pyrénées
19 pl. du Général-de-Gaulle
64220 Saint-Jean-
Pied-de-Port
59.37.01.01.
Service until 9 pm.
Closed Monday evening
(November–March),
Tuesday (exc. summer).
Cards: V, AE.

Jean Ramet
7-8 pl. Jean-Jaurès
33000 Bordeaux
56.44.12.51.
Service until 10 pm.
Closed Saturday, Sunday;
Easter week; August 10–24.
Card: V.

Saint-James
Jardins de Hauterive
3 pl. Camille-Hostein
Bouliac
33270 Floirac
56.20.52.19.
Service until 10 pm.
Open daily.
Cards: V, AE, DC.

La Tupina
6 rue Porte-de-la-Monnaie
33000 Bordeaux
56.91.56.37.
Service until 11 pm.
Closed Sunday.
Card: V.

Vanel
22 rue Maurice-Fonvielle
31000 Toulouse
61.21.51.82.
Service until 10 pm.
Closed Sunday,
Monday lunch; August.
Cards: AE, EC.